99 Voices, 99 Lives
County Poems of Iowa

John David Thompson

First Edition, First Printing

PALINDROME PUBLISHING OF IOWA
Pella

Manufactured in the United States of America
ISBN: 978-0-9720-7173-4
Library of Congress Catalogue Number: 2004098286

Palindrome Publishing of Iowa
Pella, IA

E-mail author at: statepoetpro@yahoo.com
for book sales, signings, and readings.

Manufactured by Sheridan Books, Inc.

To Iowans, Everywhere…

I am a line man for all counties,
and I push a proud pen.

Before most of you met your first morn,
I was born in one of them.

Goldfinch greets me at easterly window.
The rose and I grow in a ditch reserved for the wild.

Among the strongest of vines there,
Iowa's child.

This poetry project is a fusion of two passions:

Iowa History & Poetry

Special Thanks To

John Liepa,
Iowa History Professor, DMACC, Ankeny, Iowa

&

Billie Evans,
Language Arts Teacher, Lamoni, Iowa

Thanks to the folks in Maquoketa, and Pella, Iowa

In Memoriam
November 13, 1942

Bird of giving cools to plate.

Offshore—ported *Juneau*, a tin drumming.

Brothers Sullivan are down five.

All Iowa, a grave.

Come wreath season, Christmas is numbing.

December 28, 1846

Winter stars are first candles we see.
We guest homesteaders —
We children of the Territory.
Christmas, as our families attend it —
Three eves past.
We've boxing to do — colors and wraps.
Our men are in Mexico, guiding a war.
We've snow up to our souls;
And the knee shakes of more.
The year is about to take to sleigh,
Bids sleepy plows beneath — warm, idle night.
It leaves behind one last package —
Admission to the Union, to Iowans' delight.
The meadowlands, a white card;
We pioneer forms have our histories to inscribe:
Between observed birth of Our Savior
And fresh calendar's first day,
Iowa pushes the coldest of irons to become a state —
While the rest of the nation is on holiday.

TABLE OF COUNTIES

Money Talks
An Adair County Poem

The Last Rebel of the Civil War foiled,
Jesse James stages front coach to first-class snobbery,
to execute Plan B of this,
the West's first train robbery.

I am a fistful of currency
in the palm of Jesse James.
B-r-r-r! It may be
hotter than Hades,
July 1873, in Casey,
but it's *c-c-c-old* outside
the coin cave from
where Jesse wrested me
on this train.

Cash-napped, clip-cracked —
What could be worse
than to be snatched
from your cache
inside accessorized purse?

Pilfered of dignity,
demoted to loot,
my money is on Jess
to break away   clean
of this unscheduled crossing,
free finger and boot.

Oh, I suppose
my tender can port
the bastard and boys
to Missouri. Too bad —
he and Frank thought
they had gold's weight
to gain. *Man!*
I prefer Madam's
perfumed hand.
You bandits aren't
getting any Younger!
And, shoot, there's
shenanigans in Cheyenne
to blame!

The Shining
An Adams County Poem

A Hollywood reduced —
one star, one door.
Just whom would
that glitter-knocker
hang for?

H-e-e-r-r-r-e-e's a clue!
A no-name introduction
drips from sidekick lips of McMahon.

H-e-e-r-r-e-e's another!
A minstrel Doc behind a what's-up curtain,
stetho-trumpets *Tonight's* band.

H-e-er-r-r-e-e-'s a third,
Nicholson's Jack Torrance pans to his Wendy,
in the Kubrick film, the comin'-lovin' of an axe.

Parr and Allen, seek retirement's groves.
Let the Kid from Corning
take a whack.

He is REDRUM (murder)
on late-night upstarts,
can-we-talk tarts, red-eye apprentices.

Kid Post-Prime-Time whips 'em,
forwards, sdrawkcab (backwards),
eats their cancelled toast for breakfast.

From the northwest corner
of 13th Street and Davis,
to Studio 6-B, Carson sawed monologues
before sending a smiling America to sleep.

Who better to baby-sit television's boom-babies?
What finer stunt-and-skit brother to keep us?
Beyond that one star, one door —
a mirror strewn with Angie Dickinson kissing-stick:

R A T S R E P U S   (SUPERSTAR)

Gilded Woods
An Allamakee County Poem

God is an exalted painter;
Heaven, his exultation of paints.
A spill to the earth and lo!
West to East—atypical rivers, ablaze—
Turkey, Upper Iowa, Volga—
When dry, their beds, honeyed breath
Of stone grain.

I walked among Little Switzerland's
Vault of gilded woods,
Along tawny bluffs of hickory, pine.
The endangered jeweled shooting star
I ambled to meet.

Will her crown cast deep lavender or snow white?
Does my pursuit know the Sky she flowers for—
Fades in effigy
Beneath the deer's evanescent feet?

Sun-dappled glades—

When creating this,
The Yellow River and Forest,
God, Immaculate Vincent,
Must've been working
As close to Sunday
As the *Scriptures* would allow;
For that's when I like to think
He would choose fall's gold suggestions,
To enamor Mother Nature's tog,
Her starry, starry gown.

Shine of saffron, driftless, all around me—
Why, it's even ocherous, full amber
In the beasts' burial of shade.

A ripple yodels,
Here it rains! Here it rains!
Grab a quench of leaves, parched chum!
Imbibe the Lord's provide of lemonade.

A Chief When a Child
An Appanoose County Poem

This Congress I address,
You men of territories, states,
Eloquence asks onto you:
Do my feathers make me a bird?
Must my people and I migrate
Deeper into dry tongue of the desert —
Far from milk of Mother Mississippi
To where our moccasin steps,
Ancestral breaths are unheard.
Expansion and purpose
Are Nothing to the Sauk and Fox
But a cavalry of smoke —
Dragoon's powder and gun.
Restive day will come, white leaders,
When the coal pitched in my soul
Ignites, Inquires,
Not so much to where
Does the native foot turn,
But how fast does its spirit run?
And you who settle upon our dust
Cannot remove the foundation of injustice done.
How do I know such fate as true?
Why, I was born brave, yet beguiled.
I am Appanoose —
In presidence since a papoose,
A chief when a child.

Plow in Oak, Oak in Plow
An Audubon County Poem

Breaking up our team, man and beam, like soil,
  he releases my handle of rustic duty.

In the custody of limbs,
  I pardon him, my farmer, to serve troops' call of Civility.

His button-hand soars
  to dress Union shirt sowing freedom's path

to bring glory
  north and home, from brother's bloodied grass.

Exira's winters rust harsh;
  I drift to inanimate life —

and still — I wait and weave the seasons —
  like long-suffering wife.

My blade roots deep.
  Come spring, tree cuts new leaves.

Longing in place,
  we suffer from the disease —

plow in oak —
  oak in plow —

symbiotic shade of grace,
  plod and shroud.

Old Wood, take my last shine, bury me.
 My edge rests its dreams, less and less, I see —

a world of care, a world of peace — chance —
my farmer home to handle me.

Braille Bytes
A Benton County Poem

I BRAILLE ROAD CROSSING:
LOOK OUT FOR THE STARS

Said the Braille letter *A*
to the Braille letter *B*,
Do you feel what I feel?

Upon our raised plates of gold,
Are you with us letter C?
Do you feel what we feel?

A finger, a thumb —
Someone's first-day-of-school son —
Learning has him by the tactile tongue.
Let us listen to what the child's mind can see.

Anytime, anywhere,
answered Braille letter *A*.
Become celestial, boy,
besought Braille letter *B*.

Correction, crowded Braille letter *C*.
Celestial is the catalyst-gift from me.

Braille Bytes

II BREAKING WAVES

Three barefoot boys
in a bottlomless boat christened,
named *Blind Faith* —

they don't need
sight of sun, nor direct of wind, to know belief
flows one way.

Surely, it's Deity
to bless these three, when vision's pupils
oft have failed —

where Cedar bends
her bluest limbs and, prow to aft, Danger's
drafts set sail.

Along concern's shoreline —
Vinton patrol, a pool of school officials,
test worried waters

of their minds,
then all fears recede
like guided tide.

Go-Fish for miracles —
you'll never catch such
a record-breaking tale.

River, o, river,
turns a primer of steel, poignant waves
made of Braille.

Three barefoot boys
in a bottomless boat christened,
named *Blind Faith.*

— for the Fettys,
Jack, Mary, Kent, Jane, & John

Portraits of Chief Black Hawk
A Black Hawk County Poem

I PORTRAIT OF CHIEF BLACK HAWK

I am sitting for my portrait,
Unorganized Territory, the frame.
I won't look white flash in its thunder,
but gaze ever eastward, toward Lost Mississippi,
home waters, I one day will reclaim.
My cheeks are primed in oils,
my sorrows stroked in rain.
The brush is still before the war.

Picture it, or paint.

Where are the Sioux and Winnebago?
If Ioway brothers were posed for mockery,
my model cry would die to save their names.
I know return to Illinois will lead to purchase,
but idle squat will do the same.
Sauk tongue is spitting image—extinction, I distaste.
I am sitting for my portrait,
the masterpiece fitting for signature shame.

II DESCENDANT OF CHIEF BLACK HAWK/OVER BOTH BARRELS

When I was born into this Sauk tribe,
the hand that blessed me spoke an oracle,
You will follow the sun,
it prophecized in settling my birth.

I stepped toward manhood, one territory at a time,
knowing not what rises east, but what forces west.
Dust of blood, shame-blown negotiations,
forked-tongue of authority—these settled, too.

Up country, beyond the eagle's breath,
fell shadow of Chief Black Hawk, my brother
feathers down a warrior's last span
over the remains of his Waterloo.

Without him, we are a river run dry,
a creditor never to receive his due.
Without him, the deal is white,
and firm palm shake, skewed.

Portraits of Chief Black Hawk

Now, I no longer step, I moment-stand,
a man dispossessed over both barrels.
I am told to be passive, receive for all this land,
exchange of one ration of tobacco, one lot of salt.

Black Hawk looks down,
a dark pillar.
This offer, these lies — divide, he reminds.
Greed balances both sides of the fault.

Outfoxed by the feds,
I turn and go to what I know —
The West, rival of my prime.
Its wagon wheel of searing maize basks in my decline.

O, shoeless pioneers,
I join your quiet walk —
settling the prophecy
as told at first sun.

Smoked and bitter like both produces at last payment,
I reserve all thought
until the Secretary of State or my conscience
commands me to halt.

I promise my perished, my people,
to obey the calling of one.

Glow Depot

A Boone County Poem

Wet, hoarse, from completion of chores,
she lends me her wind, instinct,
warning of words.
Scant light has never shone lesser doubt.

Witness of storm, trestle torn,
she is Mercury the messenger
who must deliver quick speak
of unspeakable account.

I, her sidewick, hang in furious night.

Calmed by her courage,
I kindle what I can.
We cross what carriage remains.
My scout crawls on high ties- - -three-feet apart.
A struck tree of rolling roots barrels our way,
then falls beneath her knees and my flame.

At last, the spoils of Des Moines River behind us,
I clear fire-eating throat,
but not these wicked rains.

She gathers drenched skirts at what must be called shore.
We head for Moingona Depot, near midnight,
with nothing but Impossibility to mount.

Oncoming passenger train, soon, smokes to a stand-steel.

Haloed by darkness, in heroine's hand,
candle of rescue, wick of siege —
I am Kate Shelley's dowsed lantern,
alive, through a child's burning eyes,
saving lives, when urgent frame exclaims,
Four crew men are down, and Honey Creek Bridge is out!

The Buck of Wapsipinicon River
A Bremer County Poem

December sky, blue sleigh, flaked gifts to bestow,
the Buck of Wapsipinicon River alights the snow.

Antlers of nonpareil, six-point symmetry crowns his head.
The forest bull speaks nostril-steam, another hunter's climb fails to render him dead.

In Buck Creek, at first-grade show-and-tell, *That deer, that deer* —
a lad's hands barge for banks of Mississippi, Missouri; current story swells.

Watching pots dream of cooking the meat; town walls imagine the substantial mount.
Point and score, point and score — the publicity, the count!

A stalked legend since the birth of millennium,
every bow, shot, muzzle, and licensed foot shadow to devour him.

The sight of the white-lighted sage dripping warm sips of blood
against the tear of the moon and tear of buck stub

keeps the most corpulent trackman hungry, his fettered desire
to baste the beast skewered above winter's appetite hour.

How does Buck elude them? Where can such a tail duck and hide?
When stars see all and the call of each creature below him, a turncoat, a spy?

Then, into first firs of most offering wood,
an amateur cap brims upon him — frozen like oncoming fright trains, both stood.

Silent our Buck — *Boom!* went the nearby town. *A prize like no other!*
Until through the boasters' parade, one yearling stammers looking for his fell mother.

Independence Mental Health Institute
A Buchanan County Poem

If I had been here,
it was for holiday,
a visit, a dalliance
brief respite bidding
friend or a loved one well.

Look in the archives.
I never registered,
simply a guest
playing croquet
on green courts
between castles & clinics,
a blue heron piloting overhead,
casting prehistoric shades
over slake roses & hostas,
a waterfall sparrow lost
from the Great Lakes,
lost & looking for HOMES.

How odd this place, Independence.
Each patient bound somehow,
helpless & free. Like a
tuna net, the institute spawns,
catches 28 counties.
Rainbow-bellied,
a pot of gold at my caudal fin,
I am the wiggler that got away.

I am back again (to visit)
today, today, today.
I knock the hour's opponent out
with the mallet that caused
a hard ball to roll my way.

The heron flies over the cuckoo's nest.
A hostile syringe coups & nips me in the bud.

Oh, Huron, Ontario, Michigan, Erie, Superior —

I am blue, downwind, catatonic; but I crack the mnemonic code — HOME.
Hope only matters elsewhere.

It is among first fires of July. Beneath my bed — prepared notes, the birth of a nation,
& mothered in pillows — Independence Day.

Painting Rembrandt

A Buena Vista County Poem

A grayscale of orphans weaned from a train,
the one street, orange scurry, fin-de-siecle flame—
all is vivid illusion, wide, enclosing space—
the bank is Baroque; some currencies never change.

Eschew of sentiment, light to the mind's touch,
signed, *Gorget of the gods, plumed cap of the Dutch*—
a lame rake is dancing, leafed duck on a crutch—
table of travelers who don't get around much.

A sun with no shoulders, piggy backs rain,
the town's one window, a landscape, indubious pane—
a painter drinks the don't-water, despite quarantine fuss—
he gives his spool of tools the usual brush.

It's a good view, good view.
The folks in Old Madrid—well, they'd agree, too.

The Whole County Did It
A Butler County Poem

White-gloved, on duty for 24x24 miles,
Butler County stands in the doorway
as Detective Dumont enters the Parkersburg drive.
There's been a killing in Kesley,
& the birth of an Allison alibi.
Criminal, culpable prints the Clarksville pages.
Aredale blows its steam amiss.
Greene's a yellow-journalism of rages.
Throw him the book, Bristow vehemently breathes.
Send him Sinclair, Packardl!
Aplington applies to the consensus,
This was murder made to order in silver-service degree.
The smoking gun was found cooling in the Cedar.
All Austinville tall-Texas talks
of bullets embedded in, where else, Shell Rock.
New Hartford, too, has a heart of granite.
Send the hired help to jail longer than Grassley's been in the Senate.
White gloved, relieved of duty,
Butler County stands coiffed & cuffed.
Oh, those finger fits may be clean enough;
they couldn't be whiter
as our pantryman pours the heat a glass of homicider.
Whodunit? Who me?
His index of innocence may point to himself
as if disbelief forbids him to answer
hard knock for the reprehensible, reprimanded;
but Butler's white gloves, fingered, red-handed.

Manson Killer

A Calhoun County Poem

June 28, 1979

The wind is down; the air found still
A picnic sky lays down its knives
As if it had an evening to kill
Comes an assassin to Manson
From calm ceiling-sea,
Comes F4 funnel, rubble
Death's debris,
Toll of three—
And you
Thought
Chuck
Only
Kil-
led

HOLLYWOOD CELEBRITIES

Ascent of the Blackbird
A Carroll County Poem

The shine of the blackbird banks over fires of France.
I lift grit-spirit to witness its glean ascent.
White face of coffin downs my last bone with last breath.
Such is death by wing-and-wink at a soldier's glance.

First coup de grace—Ghost Chain, serve bete noire for my haunts.
I feel your company rust laced between feet spent.
Oh, home folks, Glidden, my stone, my sentry, my tent—
Forgive war's ingénue world, the debutante's lance.

Blackbird, he darkens, at slow approach of quick light.
The matinee sun, a fleur-de-lis, sparring knight.
I've no tick to battle such portents, cold and sprawled.

Time is a tinkering doughboy about to die.
Mom's sweet rolls, store—in Des Moines my own road and mall—
Enough to adieu blackbird with a single sky.

-for Private Merle Hay and family

Voices From the Iowa Underground Railroad, I and II
A Cass County Poem

I THE OTHER HOUSE OF HITCHCOCK

Dial F for Freedom

No rail, no road,
this ground under—

Sandstone on a hill, Lewis, Iowa,
south by southwest—

Shoofly bates its wing,
rears first window of air.

Like virtually every character
in Norman's psychosis—

a lunchtime affair with a man named Sam,
boss' stash-bottle of office brew,

by the time you leave from Phoenix, Marion Crane,
a client's $40, 000,

hotel guest who used all the cold blood
and hot water in the shower,

moth-eaten mother
in the company of a single fly,

yes, every stowed-soul, Negro, here—
from Nishnabotna's banks to Bleeding Kansas—

everyone at Hitchcock House
has something to hide—

each disciple of flying geese
on drunkard's path relief.

Behind fruit-cellar cupboard, tuck-away, basement,
someone called the new baby *Peach*, her mother *Tree*.

Hope is hindered, huddled dark,
but, still, John Brown, she thrives.

Behind this fruit-cellar cupboard,
jarred, tight lids,

prize-winning preserves,
human lives.

II CRACK OF BLACK WALNUT

Crack of

      black walnut

along stealth's

        way to

           Shell-House—

           Worried, its

fallen, bruised

           skin seeks

        reprieve

in God's

        vigilant snow.

Hooverville
A Cedar County Poem

Not exactly a nightingale singing in Berkeley Square, is it?
The ash and ache photograph of a Hooverville near a reservoir
deep in the bleed of Central Park.
And don't forget the shantytowns erected along Highway 66
from Mississippi to Bakersfield—
strewn like bits of Wall Street ticker-tape waste,
Hoover blankets, Hoover Pullmans—
his name a Proper Adjective for anything *ruinous, bad, depressed*—
1929 prohibitive, hung over, unemployed,
its undernourished body distended into the 1930s.

Boy, I can see him now, through rose-colored—no—
make that Depression glass.
Young Herbert, Bertie, growing up among prairie grasses, modest cottages—
between Main and Downey, son of a blacksmith, mowing the mayor's lawn,
hanging a horseshoe like a yuletide wreath over a widow's back door.
Son of a Quaker, orphaned, by age ten, to Oregon.
He is a manhood away from his engineer mastery,
a dozen love letters from the one Stanford-stamped to Lou,
several appointments away from Oval environs, a nation's mood swing away
from being despised and adored.

Hoover called the Great Depression a *transitory paralysis*, but them's fightin' words
to farmers throwing milk and fits onto Devil's Highway, bread line queued to next county.

So America engineered a few false attributes, built a great wall, to the truth about Hoover—
Hoover the Diplomat rescued Chinese children, during dragon rounds, Boxer Rebellion.
We *au revoired* the fact Hoover the Humanitarian saved, brought home
thousands of tourists from beleaguered France.
Our tastes waffle at the idea:
Hoover the Keeper of Good Commerce fed the entire country of Belgium—
when Brussels was overrun by the Germans,
had no francs in its pants.
Even environmentalists casted doubts about Hoover the Conservationalist—
but he cared, indeed, about our ecology—down to the last salmon.

During post-WW-II reconstruction, Democrat Truman didn't give him hell;
he gave Republican Hoover, a top job.

Scapegoat, scholar, rumored to be British,
Hoover knew the presidency was a shrewd, elusive bird,
so he took no seed-pence for it. Not exactly a nightingale—whistling away—
but a hard-luck meadowlark caught in a spare-dime cage.

Indeed, they were hard times, but, America, you'd be hard pressed
to find another like the West Branch wonder—first in flight from California to West Wing—
who, when he vacated a table of many hats,   left a room of empty seats.

Death of a Music Man
A Cerro Gordo Poem

Packaged and bowed,
pink and red,
French silk, chantilly lace,
attached crinoline
cascading over sleeveless
party dress,
she tests the waters
of Surf Ballroom, Clear Lake, Iowa,
alone.
Where is her beau, this Cupid's evening?
Only River City and America know.
Seventy-six dark horns blow.
For whom? It is her deluded guess.

Valentine's Day, 1959,
a Saturday at that —
not even a fortnight has passed —
since a stubble field north of town
transformed to a single-engine grave,
early shiver February 3rd,
why even the groundhog has heard —
that'll be the day, his last.

Beachcombers in tuxedoes offer a slow turn;
the girl in pearls saves dance card for him,
waves them ashore, shakes her head a slight no.
A Marian tries to reference the lost lass,
Bobbie Sock, where have you been?
Don't you hear the down-drift beat,
slide of music's death in trouble snow?

Our Miss tucks his bluebonnet boutonniere,
traveling Texan, buries it in her stood-up hand —
then, a rival ingénue points at only-lonely's
vacant corsage breast.
La Bamba lives through air;
the crowd, like Waylon Jennings, catches its lucky breath.

Miss Lovelorn taps random shoulders,
Have you seen him, his rhythm guitar?
He was to pick me up hours ago in Mason City
in an ermine-lined car. I swear
the Beechcraft reached Fargo.
We all dug him, next night at Moorhead.

Some cruel cricket strings in open ear,
P.S. He's dead.

Death of a Music Man

Death of a Music Man

She gathers remains
of her oceanfront heart,
escorts the brittles outside,
time for pop-culture's wallflower
to rinse overture's foam.

Good night, my someone.

With a sudden urge for pie,
and good ol' American girl cry,
Peggy Sue waits at Eternity's Curb
for Buddy Holly
to swoon and carry her home.

Cherokee Lullaby
A Cherokee County Poem

No dreams, warns the Cherokee mother,
her nocturnal gaze, brave, a shadow cloaked
over the shoulders of Gemini children,
sky a swaddle of stars. She cups
her hands like half-prayers,
possible moons, cup and lifts
the chins of the dispirited pair.
Son, the air names you Trail;
and, daughter, the wind calls you Tears.
Blanket of willow, covers twin gifts,
from lips down, fictive weave,
a blessing for tight, sallow slumber,
cousin of the shadow, free of color
or creation of somnambulant wonder.
Her own eyes sighing dust,
duct dry, flood of sorrow.
The Ozark Plateau lies level ahead,
but nothing evens tomorrow.
No dreams and no dreaming.
This is Hell only because we can dream of Heaven
the white man never returned and forgot to borrow.

Won't You Marry Me, Hill?
A Chickasaw County Poem

The only guest
at the her shower is God.
She tells him,
For my gift,
let your rains paint me blessedly white.
Her walls have studied
the anatomy of the wedding gown
to each detail, delight.
She knows the custodian's abandon
escorts out the last
of congregate Sunday afternoons—
leaving her to catch lone bouquet-ray,
Sabbath's dying light.

Lady registers at all Nashua newsstands
an eight-piece setting of *now*,
a centerpiece of *soon*.
Wildwood dale, be the pastor;
Borrow, the groom.
Blue bells, comes the bride
drawn at the waist
by the weight of cathedral tombs.

Her train is a lawn of pressed lilies
patience has grown
with the witness of water
and shade's stoic trill.
Sachets of scented rice
perched like lovebirds
on each window sill.

The Little Brown Church in the Vale
prepares to marry—

                                    but she never will.

Rural School Comin' Down
A Clarke County Poem

The tales about them seem to *s-t-r-e-t-c-h* like old porch boards
with each telling by a parent, grandparent, or relative still living.
The distance, never spoken without *great* or *long* as precedents,
without the regaler's hands reaching from living to dining-room partitions,
lengthens about a mile each year. The height of snow drift in winter
rises from ankle to shin to knee to waist-deep.
And the tone is a nostalgic moan with gaping, sonorous *ooohhh*
somewhere in the testimony for respect and pity.
You kids today just don't know how good you have it!

They're becoming extinct, you know—not kids today,
but those one-room, makeshift, rural schools
like the theoretical 108 that aligned 12 townships here—
unused barns, chicken coops, wagon sheds, some new proppers
planned on a grid, a cut not unlike brownies or marshmallow squares,
the treat, the privilege of education served by a schoolmarm,
known as Dame, who had the strictest parents, the P. T. A.

She had to be home by 8 PM unless poised at a school function.
Her petticoat was doubled, not her salary, which was often
provision pay in the form of corn, flax, oats, hay,
brick, iron, and other farm-product wage. Dame was not
to keep the company of men, ride in their vehicles
unless they steered with the license of *brother* or *father*.
She stoked the stove's fire by 7 AM daily,
so the children reaped warmth from first-hour frost.
Miss could not marry, leave town, let her hair down
without permission, or loiter in the town's ice-cream shops.

Completion of eighth grade an achievement, a test
of attendance, acumen, and state requirements.
Penmanship was, of course, a skill of study.
You worked for your marks, didn't cop from a buddy.
The quick brown fox jumped over the lazy door
was a staple sentence, for its declare contained all letters
of the heavenly alphabet. You added, subtracted,
sang, carved, laughed, grammatized inside the same modest four walls.
History wasn't a course; it was in the making.
You would never forget it.

Toilets limed with cakes, a washstand gurgled guard outside the hall—
no security checks, study periods, passes, or open hours.
A flag, a pump occupied the yard. No separate desks—
sticks between logs, wedged to the structure's side, sticks with planks
for inkwells, buttonhooks, pen knives, and basket-shaped lunch boxes.

Rural School Comin' Down

Townships with a secondary population of rural schools—

Madison	Washington	Fremont	Liberty
Troy	Ward	Osceola	Jackson
Doyle	Knox	Green Bay	Franklin

In theory, each of twelve townships had nine.
Which was one yours? Buzzard Roost perhaps,
where the wild boys swarmed? Does its still stand?
Oh, where have you gone, our harridan marms?

My own mother, Little Marjorie, attended a one-room pitch,
next door in Union County.
See her there, bow in hair, primer book in both eyes,
dust on her knees from pledge and prayer.
How lovely she looks in simple gingham.
She knows by rote—arithmetic and the road.
Goin' home, goin' home, her travels bend old.
How lovely she looks at lesson's descending.

So many of them are comin' down, rural schools,
like Sunday morning in the Kris Kristofferson ballad.
Some by erosion, atrophy, storm, legislative plow—
a depreciation unappreciated.

I guess I was born too late, rural school.
I'd like to keep you upright, preserved,
give you a hand, best bell of the land.

Ah, shucks! Just my luck!
I flip an Iowa quarter in mid-air of despair
and—wait an Arbor Day minute!
Tails! Reverse side!
Not the hog, cow, corn, or bean—
but you, rural school, the foundation of state pride.

There, unstretchable tale,
in minted silver you stand.

—for Marjorie Thompson

Bogenrief
A Clay County Poem

Time is never up, child; it is down to you and me.

A séance summons innocent air.
Come-hither winds tether. A soul abides.
Awning drips, late-summer rain.
The mat spells not a welcome, but gathers, *Why Wonder Why?*

A widow enters scarlet chambers,
bent and blown, her translucent frame ignites
like the Tiffany lamp on table,
brimmed with boucle lace and cups of white.

Upon its light—Parisian panels, glass seascape in relief,
stone beach, suspended ferris wheel taunts Medusa's tide.
Outside hush-walls, the town's county fair, true-blue carnival attractions,
oblivious to this, Madam Spencer's ride inside.

The door seals second thought.
Hesitation, but stained remiss.
Smoke and fog are uninvited,
yet present company is kind to fraud and mist.

Hostess speaks, *I am your velvet vessel.*
You seek an answer for the wounded dance.
Approach. Do not bother to dust your dress for dollars.
Child, you have paid for this pain in advance.

The lamp turns a shade of gypsy rose,
its stand a trellis, thin-fingered thief.
Widow is an open hand,
chaired in wonder and belief.

Anchored in her anguished world,
above, the dead-beloved   boat-by in a fleet of dreams,
the mourned and the missed,
eclipse dried leaves of tea.

A spirit drips from medium, face of boucle lace;
it lips in prompted tongue. All palms forget their rehearsed lines.
Bogenrief centerpiece becomes an aged umbrella of uncolor.
Widow wipes a wet afternoon from her eyes.

Final gesture is sentient penance.
Fallen shawl comforts floor from beveled knee.
The lamp, alas, is broken art,
bogus-sold in separate chambers of bone and grief.

Guttenberg: Pearl Button Workers' Strike by Land
A Clayton County Poem

Guttenberg Press — In print

Buttons on the sea!
Thread a catfish in the eye —
Pearl to purl! From here to Muscatine!
Throat-strokes the fore oar —
Ashore, pickets flick stones —
Workers steamboat mad
At the Mississippi mermaids
Sweat-shopping obediently —
Negotiations on the shell —
If union strike by land,
Use the buxom subs finned
In tangerine-green —
Rivers-a-nymph!
A freshwater factory —
Shiver-in-a-glimpse —
What a clam-ity!

In Old New York
A Clinton County Poem

Start treading the mills
I'm laboring today
I want my own punch card for it
The Lumber Empire of New York

Changing these ferryman's shoes
For a plane-boarder's wage
I'll be the push & cart of it
In Old New York

I want to break wood in the township
Where the sawdust never sleeps
To find I'm King of the Mill
Cash lath of the leap

These Chippewa Basin blues
Are pining away
I'll be the baron's bark of it
Come on, New York

If I can trade timber there,
I'll be one of seventeen-million millionaires
Cream of my crew — it's up to you
Before Clinton, New York

Mrs. Milk and Cookies
A Crawford County Poem

Long before housewives were desperate, prior to
braless Maude Findlay's liberating Florida, American audiences,
Denison's Donna Reed, television's acting treat,
donned an apron upon direction, add ensemble, stir — wa-la! Donna Stone!

Bellwether of the Bouffant, Beauty before Comfort, Curator of Calcium —
Tell me your troubles, dear. I'll fry them up in a pan.
Wholesome as bread, decent as rain. They don't make Nielsen moms like this anymore.
Reed was the portentous *excuse me* to the burp of Roseanne.

Mopping her kitchen in Hillsdale — wearing house coat, high heels —
No, that's not steak for dinner, kids. It's steak, lamb, and fish!
Her living room never tumbled to vulgarity, nuclear-family treason.
She, the soprano of reason before Laura Petrie became Van Dyke's dish.

Oh, sure, she played Lorene, Hawaiian harlot in *From Here to Eternity.*
She was also a modern-day Mary in Capra's *It's a Wonderful Life* opus.
That's not a bad 1-2 to add to you vita — besides the latter's a holiday classic;
as for the former, Donna made room for gold Daddy O, taking home Best Supporting Actress.

So word to your Weezy, Wonder Years, Carla Tortelli —
And any other Dr. Diva Domestic daring to cure viewer blues, low-ratings' fever.
On Donna's famed walk, a hand full of chocolate chips and oatmeal, raisin' swell children —
And, June, she would never name any dependent of hers, *The Beaver.*

Unhappy Hour at the Hotel Pattee

A Dallas County Poem

Murder, high tea,
at the Hotel Pattee—
Actually—
the Slaughter & Sipping spree
occurred across   the street
at the Thymes Remembered.

Our suspect fled
the scene there,
jay-ran past
a bell of Willis Avenue boys,
to the foot of Pat's stair
where legend
tagged him
The Ascending Assassin.

Up like weekend holiday rates, the miscreant went,
heaven-bound & hell-bent,
rooms four-walled and for rent.

How could such intrusion happen?

Was it all misunderstanding, a dream?
Or should he pick a room and a theme?
A sob camouflaged in a scene,
so the Heat could not cool and cuff him.

The Most Wanted said in soliloquy,
Let's see. Chautauqua-style was not my cup of last century.
It's too light in the Swede, and I clash with Russian or Japanese.
The RAGBRAI Room looks paved with captivity. Besides, it spokes me.

So the Pursued viewed a room with a tuba.
He crawled inside bloat's bell, waited until
the digs from Adel entered his hiding well.
Valves were shakin'—you woulduvatoova.

The posse, soon too, entered the Bill Bell Room.
Seein' that Sheriff Dallas was first brass, lead chair, best bean of his class,
his badge strong-armed matters by the mouthpiece like King Louis.
Justice blew the case wide open in three notes.
Name that criminal! Like the tune in the old game show!
Deputies turned in a herd for home.
One final random toot from a low, distant roam,
the top cop, to his aghast staff, blush-spoke,
Excuse me.

Mr. & Mrs. Wilson
A Davis County Poem

You don't see the Wilson's boy
in the Hank Ketchum comic strip—
playing games like ten little Indians
with neighbor tykes braving the cold.

In animation,
everyone is ageless.
This would have been the 60th season, straight,
the Wilson's boy belttled feet would have tracked 8-years old.

He, too, didn't care for Margaret Wade;
but not the way other mischiefs loathed her.
That Wilson boy didn't take to ruddy curls,
date or do as he was told.

Oh, why, couldn't he have been practical,
like the Sheaffer boy,
invent something big like the self-filling pen,
put choice in a pocket, genes on hold?

It is an early winter, Hillsdale, USA.
Martha Wilson defrosts a window pane, alas, no snow angel.
The earth blooms bare; memory fields everywhere.
Regret dresses Mrs. Wilson's head in feathers futile.

What were his favorite things—
lipstick? wigs? costume jewelry?
limp-wristed stereotypes like—
All Germans are Nazis who love only strudel?

The sidewalks are not safe when Dennis visits,
but the slick blonde bomb-elf moment-fits the bill
with his menace-a-minute reminders.
We all scoop for approval.

The play Indians come home for cocoa.
City plows coax their engines.
But for the Sauk, Fox, and Sioux—
left out in bleak's street, with that Wilson boy, too—

(Oh, Lord, obey THE ORDINANCE, George.)

it looks like snow…

removal

Among the Brome of Autumn

A Decatur County Poem

Among the brome of autumn
I down my wintry home,
Beak to spur, my trench unstirred,
A few hours from first snow.

A cocked gun swells, sport of smell,
I've heard declare before.
Hunter routes German pointer,
A theater for war.

Old World birds fill scenery.
Endangered, my allies,
Speak to me, so quietly,
Of death-stalk in the sky.

The grouse is a bit mottled,
But he cannot complain.
Bobwhite on look-out's tell-wire
Warns of All Saints' shell-rain.

Gestapo spots his rooster.
Brood stills as though unborn.
I alight from grace and fright
Above the standing corn.

The gauge is at the ready.
Season tolls to doom's sound.
I fall to earth, gauge my worth,
Oh, captor, of high ground.

Hunter, leave me dignity.
Remove not my red mask.
Waste not my feral being.
This is all that I ask.

Cold marksman's blade, resting shade,
Flense my warm breast apart.
Give to me clean dignity.
I, pheasant, give my heart.

The partridge sings to free me,
But I am more than free.
Celebrate on caroled plate.
I wing to fruited tree.

Among the brome autumn
I down my wintry home,
Beak to spur, my trench unstirred,
A few hours from first snow.

And the Explorers in This Corner
A Delaware County Poem

The crown, Wrestling Capital of Iowa, three-pronged, Ames, Iowa City, and Manchester.
If there be any further dispute, best to be settled by first settler, Julien Dubuque.

MAT MAYHEM IN MANCHESTER!
TONIGHT'S MAIN EVENT
TAG-TEAM WRESTLING
JOLIET & MARQUETTE vs. LEWIS & CLARK
TITLE AT STAKE—
LORD-EXPLORERS OF THE LAND BETWEEN TWO RIVERS!

It would have to be a neutral site, a non-riparian venue, no home-riverside advantage,
for the tag-team match billed, *Explore to the Floor to Be Lords of the Land Between Two Rivers.*
A prime choice for the evening's featured fray, Manchester, Iowa.
Promoters say it's a town that has a master lock, full-nelson,
on the nustle-and-muscle support required for the sport of wrestling.

Ladies and Gentlemen, announcer hawks his throat, *In this corner,*
representing the Mississippi River, weighing in at Parisian pounds,
Le Explorers Adored, Joliet & Marquette.
Imagine them, if you will, trunked in mink.
Joliet in castor, or fur cap,
Marquette sitting this one out for now—taking stool notes.

And in this corner, paddling for the Missouri drink,
weighing in at American scales,
the Princes of Purchase, Lewis & Clark.
Envision them, if you will, panted in pelts,
Captain Lewis winding through the crowd,
Clark behind him one fathom, aft-anchoring the promenade.

Dan Gable would serve as floor referee.
Yes, he would govern the event.
And why?
Because this is an Iowa wrestling poem;
Gable whistles where he wants.
Get it, guys?

Ding. Ding. The athletes navigate, test the ropes and waters—eyes look yonder.
No barbs, jabs, take-downs, no pins.
Each front man, Joliet & Lewis, spans his hands, shows largest catfish reel.
Exhausted, they guide themselves to tag respective mates.
In jump Marquette & Clark, burly pumped.
Each voices a love call, Sacajawea style, to native maidens in the audience.

The match, like the world all four explore, is one round.
Cartoonists Ding Darling, Frank Miller, and Brian Duffy
sit ringside to exhibit the final decision—
for, surely, this one is a draw.

Snake Alley
A Des Moines County Poem

THE IOWA DEPARTMENT OF TRANSLANTATION HAS CLOSED
                                                    S
DEPPILC, YLETINIFEDNI, AWOI, NOTGNILRUB NI YELLA EKAN
T
HE SLINKY CREATURE OF ITS RATTLE, PULLED THE BLUECLA
                                                    Y
NAEMUH FO TNEMTRAPED EHT. LIAT EHT YB NOHTYP KCIRB
D
ERING SWERVICES HAS INTERVENED AS WELL. BURLINGTON'S
                                                    F
A NI THGUAC SUPMUWATAC ;REDDAL A SEVRUC NOITATS ERI
C
URB. A TORTUOUS DEPLOY, SEMI-CIRCLE WORKERS GALORE,
                                                    S
.TUO GNIHT EHT NETHGIARTS OT YRT, TSAEB YWENIS EHT ELAC

34

Voices From the Spirit Lake Massacre, I and II
A Dickinson County Poem

I TOMAKNOCKERS

A tomahawk is knocking.
Should Hostess Gardner let it in?
Not by the shave of Spirit Lake's
skinny-scalp-skin.

The butt of a gun is beating.
Cause to this home-wreck effect—
the Sioux are irate as bandits
captivating the West.

Lord, it's been a harsh winter and history.
What will become
of our squatter daughters,
our Middle Border sons?

Lock your locks! A tomahawk is knocking.
Honey, it's Inkapaduta peddling vengeance to the white world.
You might say it's a door-to-door hair-curling massacre,
if there were any left to curl.

II SINGLE ENTRY: THE DIARY OF ABIGAIL GARDNER

I withheld
my eyes,
offered Brick Man
a stranger's face,
looked toward a silver line
unbinding the sky
as if it were
the string disgraced.

He put the Sioux through me—
there where I lay,
collected my body
like a parcel
of strangled love letters,
mounted a cowardice horse,   then rode away.

Dream Acres

A Dubuque County Poem

The groundskeeper
at Sec Taylor Stadium,
Des Moines, Iowa,
appears singled out,
hit by mindful brew,
doubly distressed,
strike-three, shot, succumbed.

In *dire's ville,*
his lead language spills
to I-Cub team doctor,
These apparitions of the outfield —
must be hosing me.
On the fly, their sheet-speak keeps telling me —
If you plant it, farmers will come.

Meteorite Sandwiched Theories
An Emmet County Poem

May 10, 1879 — Largest meteorite in North American history falls, 3 miles north in Estherville.
47 years later, Fred Angell invents the maidrite, a loose-meat sandwich, Muscatine County, Iowa.
The connection? Meteorites to maidrites — Gas zooms on corn, & Fast food is born.

A saga, cosmic tail—
loosely based
on vapor plate
served from counter, er,
outer space.

I UPPER CRUST THEORY

Sever Lee's farm, 1879—
Higher minds prescribe
an Angell of Heaven,
miracle of sauce and science,
crater-created zesty fireballs,
dislodged from Zeus' wrath-oven,
hurled them, heave-harp,
north of Estherville, 'round suppertime,
just as people, we produce in progress,
sat and squat to dine.

II MEATY THEORY

Pickled tongues surmise
a meteorite sandwich
embreaded the earth,
passing Saturn's onion ring,
moon's curly fry—
mustard-streaked,
ketchup blasts   on the side.

III BOTTOM BUN THEORY

More speculation rises.
Space was lonely,
a vacuum carriage,
void of marriage,
lost in a trek, in search of
a maid right for wedlock.
So enamored was he
with Earth's fair-air,
his proposal kneeled
the continent
with quite a rock.

The German Immigrant
A Fayette County Poem

She quills to her friend,
wooded and warmed in the Northeast.

Gerta, oh, Gerta, there aren't any trees.

We traveled from stagecoach
to steamboat, then rail.
We said goodbye to timber
at the Mississippi River –
frosted, still.
My youngest said it
looked like the world's
biggest strudel.
Then he looked westward
and asked,

Die Mutter, where are the hills?

In Iowa Territory, we exchanged greetings
with other Heinzes, a family from Ohio,
and Indiana clan.
All faces determined as schwarms,
possessed armies, to cease
the much-talked-about West.

Husband Frank likes it here –
walking among slow grasses,
taming the quick of the streams.

I spend most of the lantern's burn
with stars, and cut and sew
a grand blanket – tuck it away
with homesick days
in a dark chest of cedar.

Gert, I've something for your humor
to tell you.

Last night, in the sod house,
daughter Gisselle inquired of me –
why I dyed the stitch a light blue.

I told her –
To put out the blazes of prairie fire,
surely, to arrive with the hoppers
next summer.

That's why I'm to give it
the color of water.

A Tractor Is Born
A Floyd County Poem

Beneath the field once barren
as a widow at winter's peak,
wheels a seed of steel,
rotates an embryo of plow.

An acre this wanting,
for eras and ages, knows
when it's time.

Farmhand, summon the midwife.
Sky, boil some water.

The time to deliver from dirt is now.

A tractor is born near Charles City.
All blessed earth, its mother.

Who's the proud dad?
You have to ask?
Stranger, you must slick the city.
Husbandry, friend, is the father.

Geneva Talks
A Franklin County Poem

Not a yackity from Ackley —
How dare you suggest
Edgar Lee Masters' *Spoon River*
could not hold a scandal
to my wicked around-town anthologies!

I've never been a lip for gossip.
I'm all-ears; you didn't hear it from me.
No chatter-trasher finds me lingering
around the Hampton talk-tin —
panning for society's dental debris.

What's that you say — *out of wedlock,*
trial separation, something with initials STD?
Why, these phrases are cheap chalk,
back-fence talk. Such leans don't swing
with my front-porch vocabulary.

I live on Discreet Street
with my neutered purrs, Consideration & Tact.
We don't dog the fallen likes from Faulkner,
the Alexander not-so-greats,
I, and my clean-as-Carnegies house cats.

If a rumor spreads like lightning on a kite in Latimer,
well, I assure you, fellow Franklinites,
it is surely benign; and it's purely
coincidental my wordy wire is a garland
growing hemlock on its grapevine.

Anything for a Buck
A Fremont County Poem

Don't fall in love with a horse.
She'll up and leave you with the passing Mormon rain.
Go ahead. Just try to dress broncette in matrimonial glory.
Your spurs will bite first, curatorial dirt, followed by a humble-seat stain.

At the Sidney Rodeo, a sorrel will quarrel anything for a buck.
The auctioneer-announcer duels as pastor.
Give me one, make it two, five, six, seven —
Eight seconds couldn't hit the whistle any faster.

You hung in there, cowboy and chassis! What do the judges think?
Lift your ten gallon. Look at that score!
You lasted longer in the All-around than most all-human couples do.
Besides, how does a fitful hoof sign for divorce?

Eight seconds in the ring —
why the union of cowpoke and kick was worth the blender!
Throw in a set of Horse and His towels,
but I'd keep my legal tender.

Yep, not so fast, kids. Hold off on your Muttin Bustin' contest.
Billy forgot to consider his Nellie can't count.
Ah! Equestrian gymnastics! Applause a bit for booted vaulter!
There's no clowning around on that 10.0 dismount.

Ouch! You'll need a doctor, Jilt.
You rear-on-return will require a stitch.
At least your heels dug deeper
Than the usual seven-tick itch.

Berate and blame her. Detest and hate her.
That four-legged filly was born to disparage.
Wipe that veil of soot off you, chap. Engage a second saddle.

The first? She's ske-daddled and strapped on another lad.
You've been taken for a ride; your seat impeached,
long-been-had, your carriage.

Don't let the eight letters fool you, scrape.

There's no shorter *mare* than *marriage.*

How to Sway Popular Opinion
A Greene County Poem

POLLSTER OF ETERNITY
(Vote for One)

<u>G</u> GEORGE GALLUP (primacy effect, candidate's name appears first)
<u>A</u> GEORGE GALLUP (mass effect, name appears more than once)
<u>L</u> *Geroge Gallup (subliminal effect, name barely appears, imprints in the mind)*
<u>L</u> GEORGE GALLU

                   P (dangling chad effect, name lingers, wins)

<u>U</u> GEORGE GALLUP (penultimate effect, next to last, holds fast)
<u>P</u> GEORGE GALLUP (recency effect, last to show, receives the pull)

GEORGE GALLUP (summative effect, all adds up — Vote for Gallup!)

Hog Ghost Story
A Grundy County Poem

The pigs were dead, no doubt about that—
long butchered into apple-jawed roasts, holiday chops.

This is no Christmas carol.
The smell of chestnuts on the flame
will not be smelt—if such a smell
could be smelt.

The pigs were dead, no doubt about that.

It was, as jazz purists might say, 'round midnight,
at the folding farm of ne'er-do-well Benjamin Biggs
when the haunts of poor past pork-keeping practices
began to taunt him in the wig.

Farrow-furious form lack of genetic advancement—
free at last, free at last— from those malodorous lots,
the nebulous critters, vengeful and bitter,
why, their remains floated up floors
without so much a creak—
like a balloon parade of the bacon-deceased.

No doubt about it—dead were the pigs.

Ben was frilled in his late December kerchief.
(No wife to cross-dress in a 'twas-the-night cap.)
He had just laid out the morrow's evening gown,
then settled down—when the bedroom door
commenced to rap!

Yo', Ben, we know you're in there.
You might remember us in squalor and pink!
We've come presently to redress past confinement.
Oh, we've come to make such a stink!

Now, Grundy Center, quick—get a gun!
Reinbeck, best beware!
For what havoc wreaks
when gossamer grunts
take to talking and the stair.

Suddenly, his sheets seemed like an abattoir.
The troughs had turned; Biggs felt like fodder.
He lay supine, awaiting the swine
to take him away to noxious slaughter.

Hog Ghost Story

A drift of gilts, a parcel of hogs
entered his quarters by means, not unlike osmosis.
Holy! Ben cried. The trite not to be denied
when he swallowéd an octave to bellow, *Moses!*

The hogs grabbed Ben like take-out—
bad farmer to go—
slopped him into spirit—
morbid mortgage and hoe.

An insult to salt the injury—
though Farmer B's time was up—
When taking Ben's corpse down for final chores,
that shiver-me-litter used Floyd of Rosedale
                                        as a door stop.

That's the last anyone heard or saw of said Benjamin Biggs.
His farm sold, then converted into a requiem sewer.
Those pigs were dead—no rattle about that!
Why, even Marley's apparition would cowpie a pile
if he had eyed this unchained malady of manure.

Admit One Bandit to Yale
A Guthrie County Poem

Yale, IA — Pop. 287

Alert the forest,
tell the chapparal trail,
a raccoon — at last —
accepted to Yale.

His ivy apply, nothing to hide,
no record to mask.
Eyeshades made the grade,
cleaned up for the task.

Gruffish but happy,
sated and ready —
Garbage Renewal 101
his plan of study.

Our omnivore won't come to class by car.
Zorro intends to furrow.
His only residential request:
a dorm room that's hollow.

Any grub will do.
Twenty Shredders is not an eclectic thing.
Rac wants a dip in the River Diploma
and to add to his seven class-species tail rings.

Kantorville
A Hamilton County Poem

He takes a break
from the famished corn cracker
to watch a prison-inning or two—
late summer tradition,
War Between the Towns,
game of hardball,
between gray Jewell from the South,
and, to the North,
blue Newcastle-on-the-Boone.

There they are, players
of the field, behind bars,
wires, and fences,
visiting defense from the North starving
for an out; home batter
pining for states' rights
beyond the outfield benches.

It is pre-season before *Andersonville* hits the majors.

Afternoon sun is overseer;
it dispenses what nourishment it can
to hungry slider on the mound—
to those Newcastlers refusing to wear Southern gloves
upon their proud Union hands.

The game is in the Deep—Jewell—
and, like the season's sparse kernels,
the host team will not yield—
a Confederacy of Bunters—
its inhumane treatment, such beating—
unless future Websters join their side of the field.

The sole observer shakes the chaff
from disbelieving head;
Mason and Dixon offer scant concessions
in linear booth.
Then, wisdom hits our harvester on the ear.

A prisoner of winning is a *P. O. W.*, too.

Hobo Convenience Store
A Hancock County Poem

A boxcar of us fits like a six-pack—
Refrigerated, inseparable souls.
We bed newspapers, brown bags, trash plastic.
Stories we tell glaze a few donut holes.

Life's a fountain of unlimited refills.
So's, we've been dispensed like cubed and crushed ice.
You won't spot us hurtin' back in work's break room.
That's just wiper fluid gushin' down our eyes.

Hot Dog! Britt is a breath mint, come August.
The proof's in the hooch we call Railsplittin' Pop.
Our hard swallows return to cappuccino.
When sad tracks depot near Sunday blue laws.

We come and go, just like you gourmet folks.
Drizzlin' quick milk and gone-by gas on us.

Mr. State Fair
A Hardin County Poem

Imagine, if you will,
a ferris wheel spinning
in his resplendent mind.

Around his pupils
bunt blue ribbons
keeping grand eyes
on best prize.

Can you sing, kid?
Can you juggle?
Keep that fiery baton out of the aisles!

And what's better than a donated piano
mastered by sprout on the concourse?
Its gifted ivories bringing all of Iowa
to a Sunday afternoon smile.

Bill Riley, the Showman of Showmen,
at the Iowa State Fair —
the Icon from Iowa Falls —

May the ON-AIR applause never end.

He turned competition into ceremony,
and each competitor into a friend.

And I swear —
when that senior finalist
sings Ol' Man River in resounding bass —

the song must have been written for him.

Bertrand Lets Off a Little Steam
A Harrison County Poem

My sailing leaves nothing for posterity,
but my drown tells you this—
carousing in the digs of the fierce Northwest
was, not mine, but the goldminer's wish.

The Missouri River may have netted my hull,
but Big Muddy left jars of brandied cherries in tact—
tamarinds on preserve, assorted European whiskeys, some coins;
it is historical fact.

I sank quickly, like the mercury on my board—
April 1, 1865.
My graceful submerge gave all passengers fair heed;
it was God's watch of gold giving survivors sufficient time.

My down bow can *cargo* its breath forever.
Do not look for Cleopatra, Proud Mary, or me rafting the skies.
Sherman may have burned Atlanta that week,
but a river queen never dies.

Ode to Thresher

A Henry County Poem

A separate kind, thresher, I think you mean
to come to terms with western land, honest and clean.
And what you gather, what you glean
fills a nation's basket for futures seen.

Say, thresher, when the day's toil is through,
where is your wander, who is your Sue?
I could take a liking to the likes of you—
all chaff, straw muscle, strapped inside denim-blue.

As first sun harvests sky, thresher, rise and go you must
to where insecure seed clings to morning husk.
A practiced gesture by your hand, bullied thrust,
she's soon a sandwich, bread for lunch.

A pleasant mount, thresher, I think you mean
to serve you country by old-fashioned means.
But how you gather amber, love, yes, how you glean
will soon as noon be replaced by man's lust for machine.

The Almost Bride of Hayden Prairie
A Howard County Poem

He spoke,
O, my love, O, my Anastasia,
I search the jeweled revolution of your eyes
and know your Mother Russia
must be missing
her Czarina, quite.
Take my certain hand.
Take expanse, the young drift plains before you.
Happy the Slav — should you make his wife.

She sighed,
O, my love, O, kind Jaroslov,
what place is for us here
where both our people steeple not?
The Germans rise to high shadow.
French blessed the first river.
The English shake a long coat,
and the Natives are gone.

Still, fell heartland's wind
over undelivered weary.
Still, were his chances;
still, lent a faint of her heart.
He bent
to pick second-chance gesture,
quick acre of veiled prairie smoke.
When the boy rose to face her,
Mink was clear disappeared,
short-lived shooting star.

A search party reckoned,
no pack hound could scent her.
From Chester to Rochester—
not a skein of dissenter's runaway gown.

Toast of Czech chalice cut low
by the scythe of love unrequited—
out where arms cannot bear to embrace
and the farmer cannot bear to plow.

A County Seat So Small, It's a County Sat.
A Humboldt County Poem

Somewhere, there must have been a battle for it—
the claim to county seat of Humboldt County—
a contest not unlike David and Goliath as told in *First Samuel*—
id village of Dakota City versus Giant of Defiance, city of Humboldt, supersized.

Imagine thimble East versus deluxe West, each threading a soldier to stone,
to descend the Des Moines River Valley, just miles north of the watershed-ford.
Yes, there must have been a prescind, further divide, civil skirmish,
brutal Hatfield-McCoy-type feud—local politics, push of official papers—the prize.

Humboldt selects its Gulliver, Baron von Humboldt, war-seasoned, steel-winged.
Dakota City reasons, a dwarf feather, to represent, brushes of Biblical brookstone and sling.
Down to the depths of compromise, they float.
Rain is a choice-ticket witness. The Baron is rust; the feather, soaked.

Impatient sun elects prevail. Rays make way through crowded sky.
Way to flow, Dakota!
Bah-Humboldt!
Fell rust on its butt is rust, no matter the heat; but a tiny-tuft dries

to pin-cushion as county seat.

Cattle Call or Cream
An Ida County Poem

You would moo, too, if it happened to you.

The cows have come home
on family jet.
One of their own is said
laid to rest.
Ol' Esther, down hay,
ruminates her last breaths.
BovIDAe pay brisket-respects.
Fallen cudder be blessed.

The uddertaker spreads the good herd,
a calling, an aerial task.

Yes, the cows have come home
on family jet.
Charolais steer from coach.
Airedales bottle the aisles.
In loving moomery, all milk it
for one whose swoosh-tail has passed.

Back to respective pastures, heads go—
My! That service was a *teat* fast!
It may speed-of-sound absurd,
but only Holsteins reserved
a spot
in first class.

— for C. Paul Thompson

Amity of the Amanas

An Iowa County Poem

An historian told me Amity is the Sweetheart of the Colonies,
But I believe she remains its Truest Soul.
Benevolent Miss founds at no legal sundown residency.
Among concord locals is but one of possible homes.
Look for Amity's gather at tables, friendly bread.
Seek her fellowship in cellars of Welcome's wine.
She is faithful greeting on Every Street.
Good News, facing east, with gravestones, at the Lord's first shine.

Like all things, ambitious and abstract —
Amity nears Anger's domain, but there her business will not settle.
Where has Fraulein Lily gone? Gaze Iowa's Seven Wonders, inspired tourist,
Search homestead, ox-field, Rise and West, gaze both High and Middle.
Amity folds when peace is in need, of this attraction be most aware —
Constant she lives — where a heart forgives between two hands in prayer.

It's the Girl from Andrew, Sister

A Jackson County Poem

Old Hickory citizens gather at the natural bridge,
an earth-stone belvedere of limestone, dolomite, and shale—
just outside Timber City to cast a most eminent vote:
Who has been the county's most prominent person of all time?
The decision is anything but secret ballot. Pass the publicity note.

Yes, they collect among themselves, raucous and ready,
like congregate bats before shaded Maquoketa Caves—
flapping in oodles, screeching in spades.
Someone call an exterminator or zoo!
At last, the jousting Jacksonians pare it down to two.

From the 19th century, Andrew Briggs of Andrew,
first governor of our fine state.
20th-century's choice, Kim Peters, the six-player basketball guard
(phenom from the same place) who single-handedly changed
the way Iowans looked at hard-court fate.

The Girl! the unobstructed view from Bellevue.
The Governor! long throats scream from Miles.
Review her records! And she stole more hearts than passes!
Peruse his files! Homesteading, the Mexican-American War. What historic hassles!

Back and forth like an island ferry at Sabula the debate went.
Zwingle can cast swing vote;
but the Lazt City reboundz between counties, thuzly, absent.

Flummoxed, provoked, with flour orders to fill,
Get to the gist! grists powdered fists from Potter's Mill.

Just then, to everyone's tacit alarm,
the apparition of Ansel Briggs himself appears.
He intercepts the tie, his choice, clear and calm.
The First Gent of Iowa bows to a great lady by raising

one arm.

Maytag, You're It

A Jasper County Poem

I must've been the agitator.
Lord knows, she was the dispenser.

Unlike my wife,
the laundry doesn't leave.
It accumulates
like unwanted snow
this first bachelor's winter.
Crimps of denim in hapless hall,
spoiling fruits in loom —
dirt from a groundless life.

Missing a sock, I introduce myself
to the washer & dryer
pinned inside a crevice-called-closet.
Just like the wife's attorneys,
the twist nobs refuse to shake hands.

I've watched the ex-
man these machines from the
potato-couch corner of my eye —
while Favre regrouped the Packers
between downs.

I equate the process with a shampoo commercial.
Lather. Rinse. Repeat.
I separate the past from unbearable,
soak the latter in hot water
in hopes that it will fade.

The ghost of the original Maytag repairman
sits atop the top loader. His dog gone.
Lonely, famous for his pain,
retired in Lamb's Grove,
he walks about the house and strips all phones.
There won't be any calls. Get used to it, he advises.
He upgrades a filter device, disappears
into the Land of Reruns. At last,
Gilligan's Mary Ann doesn't have to wash by hand.

It is time to dry.

Loose change forms a syncopated percussion band
in the unit; it is a hard rain, but I let it pour.

Soon, all is toasty, but not forgiven.

Maytag, You're It

The laundry, no longer lachrymose,
rids its tears in a cycle of want, love, and attention.

Cheerless, I have given it my all.

Time for a clean break.

I sock the whole basket a *Dear John* letter.

Lint begs off the lid.

I ignore it with my excused shoes.

I'd like to flush the fluff down the john water.
That would take a whirlpool.

Go Newton figure.

And I fold.

Conversation with Ferris Wheel Descending
A Jefferson County Poem

Oops! The top scoop
Of my ice cream cone fell.

Clumsy. A corn dog's
More ferris-wheel appropriate.

Say, I hear they're filming
A sequel to *State Fair* this summer.

A Rodgers and Hammerstein re-do?
I declare! What will the producers call it?

Babe: In Pursuit of the Blue Ribbon —
Bill Riley and the Iowa Pork Association are casting.

Hogwash! By the weigh, did you know
The first Iowa State Fair was here, 1854, in Fairfield?

Why did officials move the event? Des Moines gets
Ever'thing — the Capitol, Drake Relays, West Des Moines.

The board changed venues because
Prize swine kept straying to Pork County.

You're pulling my turkey leg!
It might as well be Polk County.

Precisely.
Ploop!

The Smolder of Old Stone
A Johnson County Poem

Pick a plum of respite.
Pick a plum of repose.
The territory rests its case.
A state awaits Plum Grove.

Iowa City, IA, November 20, 2001 —

The University like a map is not the territory
you once blazed with fiery legislation,
the brim of a dream,
fervid promises of honest work.

This evening, abandon is a capital crime.
Fueling the news — *The Burning of Old Capitol* —
a grassfire sweeping across the Pentacrest and prairie,
from the flame of tenured tongues,
over autumn's lectern, to erudite neophytes,
who break before Thanksgiving Break,
to contemplate the smoldering of Old Stone.

It is the season of rescue;
we are all armed with water.
As your beheaded dome plunders,
Sister Heritage, this hour, loses
a tip of her golden touch.

The symbolism of a state dissipates.
Our assignment for tomorrow, symbology,
but who has time to study it much?

Knock on Wood
A Jones County Poem

Pen be discreet. Ink be couth.
Sis Nan is Queen of the Copyrights & Doc could loosen a tooth.

They are the faces
in the face of the Great Depression—
somber, iconic
marriage of the ages.
No, not farm daughter & farmer—
but artist's sister & family dentist—
both posers looking as if concealing
fresh root canals.

They are the most parodied
pair on the prairie—
caricatured as
Sean & Madonna at 60,
Garfield & the Mrs.,
Skeleton & Skeletina,
golf groupies with bag, balls,
themselves sporting gas masks.

In real art, she is marooned by isolate apron.
He impaled by pitchfork ghosts—
Our Mona Lisa of Middle America
& Her Man of the Salmon's Gib.
Funny, the longer you look
at the bloomless union inside gothic frame—
how closely resemblant
each countenance is—
like pet owner & pet.

Couple of catatonics, beaverboard buddies
two in a terrible trance—
Nan's cameo borrowed
from 1929s *Woman with Plants.*

They sprung like thresher's wheat
from the Antioch School of Regionalism,
& now hang out, well-winded, institutionalized.

Sweet home is Chicago.
Stoneses who no longer must keep up with the Joneses.
Gusty move, took the whole house with 'em.
The gabled window still points upward,
perhaps the portrait's only leaven—
to remind grounded dreamers—
Iowa is halo-fodder, but not quite heaven.

Ache, Woebegone, Daze
A Keokuk County Poem

Inflect the place's phrase
as a whining interrogation, and
at town's edge—
What Cheer, Iowa,
spreads the world's largest
psychiatric couch.
Here, the disconsolate,
the lugubrious,
tell the welcome sigh-sign
their troubles.
Serotonin streams from Skunk River
to a dry bed.
Norepinephrine,
dopamine trickle
to a tricyclic halt.
Happy has been banned.
How are you?
Ask it and you are fined.

Say, what cause, What Cheer,
for such dolorous decline?
Opera House is a dirge.
Is that a Thornburg in your side?

The tears, the tears are ancient here.
For upstream, encroach of English River,
pulled Chief Keokuk and sulking Sauk
to Kansas

with its white tide.

German POW at Algona Camp
An Kossuth County Poem

Homesick for Hitler,
Private Blue Eyes dreams
he is axis-packing the cardboard cases
at the branch-camp assembly line
for hygienic accessories —
just northeast of Algona.

American denim, distaste, on his bones,
he swears on his swastika heart —
he'll get out; he will.
His soul, like his back's fabric,
coarse and twill.

He could've chosen
from a number of Herculean labors, here —
braid hemp at the main plant;
cut timber and pulp, up-star in Minnesota;
can a record crop of peas; mind the nursery;
sheet brick and tile; do silo construction;
process milk; detassel hybrid corn;
barrel vinegar-vegetables;
clear the scrub trees from drain ditches;
eviscerate and clean Dakota chickens.

Berlin boy is looking for his Cerberus,
the work of the hound from Hell.
He selects to attach parts, a division
of boxing and shipping —

the blondes-only shift.

Kraut connects hose to nozzle-head of a thousand holes,
then showers the late-nacht foreman with bribes —
a stash of Warsaw cigars and lederhosen that fits.

Then, Blue Eyes, makes his dreams come true
and, privately, labels the final box of the final hour:

DIRECT TO AUSCHWITZ

Civil Bells
A Lee County Poem

August 5, 1861

A bit of a footnote for the state,
I, Lee County, nevertheless, believed
mine was to be a dip for Civil War neutrality.
Oh, I built my fence, neighborly white;
but it was for traditional show,
peaceable conformity. Now,
my rebellious child, Croton,
reports a brat-battle worthy of West Point,
in our backyard to me.

Mr. Lincoln,
I've a spike to split with you, sir.
Isn't it disturbing enough
most northerners think
some of your appointed civil servants
named me after Dixie's General Lee?
Why, I've dressed each of my boys
from Franklin to Vincennes
in Union blue from toe-head to knocked-knee.
I look outside my sweet, summer window,
my eyes of glory see
a carillon of cannon,
silver civil bells, from 'cross river hills,
lodged in bush, flowerbed, and tree.
A coat of gray approaches;
shall I offer them, able Commander,
some noxious ade or venal tea?

Oh, ringing noise! The horror!
My daughters Primrose and Augusta
were not raised to endure such Ulysses calamity!

Duty lies wounded in the sweet grass.
Good Annie Wittenmyer is in my kitchen
to help with the biscuits and bandages
for the broken fast of Iowa, Missouri.

Ok, I'll do it Abe, redress this miss —
But you owe me big — big as a top hat, see?
Speaking of hats, I hear Mary Todd isn't up
for the War-Between-the-States promenade,
so I throw my bellicose bonnet in for First Lady.
And I'll bring my own ball (Fire One!) to our Inaugural.
Save the last Reparations Dance for me.

Quaker Notes
A Linn County Poe m

In the 1969 Rankin & Bass
animated Christmas special,
<u>Frosty the Snowman</u>,
woolen children gather around
the yet-to-be-capped
wonder-in-white — belly-whopper
to contemplate a name
for the village's new beloved.
Tags such as *Harold*, heave-hoed —
Bruce, eight-sixed —
a kid, known in the TV credits
as Child #3
spoons the choice *Oatmeal*.
Oatmeal!?! the kids protest —
the word automatically
linked to mornings with
forced bowls of mush-stuff
spotted with termagant warts.
Piping brown sugar, mother's warm ways
could not unfreeze
the children's lumps of disgust,
sloshes in the throat themselves reminiscent
of the first polar expedition
to sight a yeti:
abominable.

Great Flood of '93
A Louisa County Poem

It was the summer
all newborn boys
were named Noah.

In lieu of traditional blue blanket,
older hands bestowed floodsplain infants
with rattle-paddles.

Ironic, wasn't it?
The one thing you could not do—
shower.

Hope on fire, Kafkaesque—
third-degree rain—
skin, burning wet.

You saw your neighbor
in another slant of light,
shared darkness.

A girl from Morning Sun—
dressed in galoshes
of misfortune—

Mock yellow,
her raincoat shook blue salt
from the sky.

A sea horse rescued her
by throwing Little Miss Levee
over one shoulder.

It was the only luck,
good or bad,
to be had.

Let It CIO, Let It CIO, Let It CIO
A Lucas County Poem

Miner, acquire that char.
Laborer, shift that tow.
Boss Frost gnaws on corn cob.
Kris and Missy toil in brisk snow.

Wonder will appease them.
Magic act taps hat of silk.
Juniors take to gesture
as Santa takes to milk.

Thump! Kid, need compensation?
Slick work conditions stink?
Minors form a union—
Joyous and Jolly, Inc.

Miner, pupil-pick at that ore.
Laborer, button that carrot nose.
Kids wage a better world
through two eyes made of coal.

Children of a Lesser Sod
A Lyon County Poem

Is this the last stop of the Orphan Train, God —
Northwest Passage out of Iowa, the final depot?

Has the state run out of heart and Heartland —
Is there nowhere else to go?

We've heard Dakota winds are wild —
Terror rides mightily through vengeful Sioux.

Can you please keep us here, Lord?
Anything Governor Cummins can do?

Are there really lions in this county?
That wouldn't be so bad,

We'd make the finest cubs —
at least, we'd have moms and dads.

A den at Inwood roars with us most excellent.
We bet Rock Rapids has a proud Mane Street — what could it hurt?

To us children of a lesser sod, us gutter swipes,
we brush-offs bound for a clean sweep of rejection's dirt.

And we've come so far, Father,
like a Nor'easter blowing in from New York.

We know tiny tongues should not car-by-car complain
on westbound train when the conductor is Our Lord.

But we've taken a liking to Iowa — place us out
to the squats who gave us scarves and fruit.

If it's good enough for corn,
why can't we, new family tree, take acre and root.

We'll say our prayers on the hour,
read the *Children's Bible*, stop sucking nervous thumbs.

This our pledge, God, as we stand on this choose-me caboose,
throwing to our lost parents, a last station of crumbs.

What's Heating Coffee Cups at the Northside Café?
A Madison County Poem

The regular crowd at Northside Café'
Stirring like sugar spoons,
Refilling old fumes.
A boil of fury whitens the morning dishes.

Hogback, McBride, Cedar Bridges—
All Winterset a-blaze!
Everyone but Robert Waller, Clint Eastwood
Said suspicious.

The uniformed blue from Truro to East Peru
Cook up the usual, dubious few.
Alas, it's all apples and scorches,
Not enough to truly commit for acts so malicious.

Oh, what be true heat to the cause
For decent folk to effect such claws,
Such citizenry injury,
Blazen and pernicious?

Peel at arson's core.
Take a graffiti graze.
Carved on burning-heart wood,
Marion M loves Red Delicious.

Mulogy at the Cemetery for the Union Crossbred
A Mahaska County Poem

Blue the lay of the Union mule.
Civil hinny resists
Tomb's gray.
For the Lord 'borts *born*
From *stubborn*.
This ass has passed,
And just death's stub remains.

The Dutch Letters of Your Mind, I and II
A Marion County Image

I THE DUTCH LETTER*SSS* OF YOUR MIND

Like a curve upon a curve
Where convex and concave meet
Holy Holland to America's Amsterdam
The perfectionary pride of Franklin Street

Savor sugar, savor spice
Neither pinch nor few grains to waste
Chill, shape, and bake until Klokkenspel chimes
Tender flakes rise gingerly to house the almond paste

Mother and daughter greet scrumptious six at Jaarsma's
Blacksmith forges one-half dozen from Vander Ploeg's
Kin folks from Knoxville speed their wheels
To grab checkered sacks to go

Like a sweet snail stationary
A tempting, slender slither into the City of Refuge
Thanks, Sinterklaas, may we have another?
Anxious clicks of wooden shoes

Domine and Mareah Scholte founded this village
Surely, on the capital *S*
Nether children learn the 19th letter
Before reciting remains of the garden's alphabet

Trumpets to tulips! Word to your windmill — more smashing than
Pella Windows — Wyatt Earp, street scrubbers aside
Nothing lingers on frontal-lobe fingers like these souvenirs
The Dutch letters of your mind

II THE GARDENER AND THE GIFT

Closing Ceremony, Tulip Time Festival, Pella, Iowa

Sunday's best-bulb tiptoes
through the High Garden.
With last sermon of spring schedule,
proper green waves betide to ebb and lift.

Among elevated staggered silver beds,
we, a ministry of outlander and native sowers,
droop our heads, offer hat and gratitude
to the Gardener and the Gift

— for the Larry Klein family

Three Centerpieces
A Marshall County Poem

I {WILD ROSE, WILD ROSE}

State Center — Rose Capital of Iowa

Wild Rose — Wild Rose
I bow to your company —
Prairie Quartz, Ditch Silk —
Pink Luxury!

To Petal, Minion Wind —
To Pasture — settle low —
Draft her virgin scent
To my unrepentant throes

Rose, threaded by thorn —
Rose, tailored to vine —
To leave you lone —
God's design.

II CENTER OF THINGS

Her folks named her Rose
for obvious reasons.
The girl's room is
at the center of things,
eye of four winds,
point of brethren seasons.

It is here, within compact walls,
where great meeting lives —
East stems with West —
Thorns of North and South forgive.

Tribes gather, too,
beside post and pillow,
to send Rose to sleep
at peace
with the equidistant world.

Ah, Rose, of fair being —
born of sun's pink-fingered complexion —
each morning, you bud, dear,
the proper direction.

Three Centerpieces

III IOWA REDEFINED

At window,
a father with firstborn—
first snowfall, winter, says,

Child, it once was thought,
most sagacious tongues taught—
Iowa meant Beautiful Land,
yet the Meskwaki word Iowa
means one who sleeps with.

One who sleeps with what, father?

Daughter, I do not know.
Beauty, I guess,
the kindest wolves of the timber,
fields a-burst with maize,
fallen roses.

And snow, Dad. Don't forget snow.

Yes, love, snow—
one who sleeps with
blessed fresh beds of snow.

Ferryspeak
A Mills County Poem

It's hard to support you, kid —
your best-laid plans.

You've got me alongside a river, idle,
unscheduled — and you don't give a dam.

I was minding my Nishnabotna business —
just fine, 'til your work and span came along.

I carried customers on my back;
and my floating tune, broke water into song.

I was cheap seats, too. A dime for a footman,
two bits for a horseman, tens cents a cow, five per sheep head.

Yes, it's a bit of a stretch to applaud you, kid.
Your nerves of fresh steel, strings of a choir, arch-defiant spread.

I can tell you've got bone, prime spine,
to take the twentieth century ridge to ridge.

This is White Cloud, Iowa, fool, long way to Long Island —
What's a ferry to do? But rue the day and pave that is building you, bridge.

Hanging with Hamlin Garland
in Watts Theater, Osage, Iowa
A Mitchell County Poem

His ghost has come to claim its Rosebud.
He has come to slip on a ruby sole.
Atlanta, he's coming to look at you, kid.
Here's to your burning.

It is 1950.   The world at breath between wars.
Ten years after his death,
I meet Hamlin Garland
in the lobby of the Watts Theatre for its premiere.
We will be evening acquaintances,
Dancing in the Dark, as it were.

Hamlin looks a shadow of his former self,
quasi-translucent, murky, milked, and sheer.

The dead don't need a ticket, but like a good seat.
Ham picks one in the middle border, eternity at every exit.
My author has missed the births of technical color,
advanced sound, and Oscars' Original Screenplay.

His eyes appear looking for stars.
He is captivated by the dust
playing like truant snow in the flicks of light overhead —
bringing film to fruition.

Garland jokes if anyone confuses him with Judy.
He died in Hollywood, successful writer, but lacking film credits.
He brings his own pad and scratch, hands me a thought.
Before Emery Slade arrives at New York, go get popcorn with salt.

We will return, he and I, Christmas Day;
the art-deco wonder will be open.
We will be ensconced and tushed in the velvet-seat fantastic.
On screen, some crazed caroler will bail
through the debts and drifts of beloved Bedford Falls.

Hamlin will pat me on the shoulder,
scratch his head with the *Coming Attractions* guide.

By George, he says,
I have missed a wonderful life.

Loess Hills
A Monona County Poem

Perhaps this is where ice comes of beauty and age.
Perchance this is where a border calls bluff, and both stoop to pray.
Or, maybe, Paul Bunyan fell from a higher plain—
Yes, maybe, these catsteps prowl his grave.

Perhaps China has a dark side to its Great Wall.
Perchance this is where moles raise the roof for an annual ball.
Or, maybe, this is where sculptors to the gods
Gather their magical clay.

The Loess Hills are everything
That old, crumbly schoolbook said they would be.
Loess Hills make silk and dirt
The same.

Ah, but these moon-cat hills,
Mount Lovelies, are not some to call
My Antonia's return to me.

You've crossed the Mighty Mo'. Haven't you, love?
You're hanging up a homestead with Nebraska's favorite son.
Silt and guilt cannot summon you to come back to me, come.

I was not Jill's chosen,
Just a tumble-tantrum *Jack*

                    falling down—

eroding

eroding

erosion....

Buxton Wonders
A Monroe County Poem

I BUXTON WONDERS

I mined, and I mind.

If I had been a settlement
where once trod
the Native tongue,

or first soil west
of catfish Mississippi
where the French dipped birth-mud,

and not a black bastion of productivity,
a living, working practice
for coal's seamless cause —

equality — where color climbed to majority,
despite the early century's
swing of Jim Crow laws,

then would state and national governments,
those white-collar power-orators
that be,

stop a filibuster moment
to preserve my place,
make a monument out of me;

"a black man's utopia in Iowa,"
unbeaten baseball teams, fair labor's dream, at last —
humanity — so it intrigues my vanished physicality some —

this ghost town asks, how discrimination picks, still exists,
among my dark ruins
set in eternal separation from the sun?

Buxton Wonders

II BUXTON STRIKES AGAIN

What did you say, man?
Boo or *batter-up?*
And is that some sort of pick
or a mitt in your hand?
You look like a haunt
who has been housing extra innings, overtime.
The ground of your hover
switch hits from a mound to a mine.
Hey, cool, your cap has a shaft-light.
I guess that's for night games.

What's that?

You're pitching for racial equality —
simple and plain.
Is that a black uniform you're wearing?
Perhaps you sport a deep farmer's tan.

Negro! Don't say *Negro!*
Where have you been, ringer?
That word is banned.

You are one multi-tasker —
ghost, lefty, coal slinger.
Why, I bet you walled away a ton,
back when you were *boy*
to every white father and son.

You know all about walls, you say?
And you have died to live for the day
when the stadium all stands together
to topple the last one.

Villisca Axe Murders
A Montgomery County Poem

Eight are waiting.

It's black as vengeance outside.
Town's electricity on summer respite.
No bugging light—except June's fireflies.
What high crimes could such bobbing lanterns
Possibly commit?

Enter, madman. All is dark—
So all is clear.
Bring your hatchet-sand and sickness
Up Joe Moore's stair.

Take the wage-man out first.
It's what he deserves
For stealing John Deere work
From the Big Man.
The children are random hide.
Blade gunner,
We've haven't the night.
Chop. Chop.
If you can't forgive yourself,
Forgive them.

Eight are fading.

Drape the mirrors and windows in death-white
As if solstice angels were here to witness.
Leave but one linger, one tip—behind:
A hired slinger needs no trigger alibi
When mass murder is blessed with time sufficient.

Exit, madman. Pass blood's port.
Take Monday's AM train.
River is quick ticket away
From mother's bath of stains.

Release the night-shift work of your fists.
With no conscience, no fingerprints.
Drop whack-weapon; it will only trail you.
Lick yourself spotless in the family's basin—
Down to the first-degree bone.
Leave me with the dead—safe at home.
I know whodunit, so this is the way I want it.
An axe doesn't ask;
It tells you.

It's the Great Melon, Muscatine
A Muscatine County Poem

Memorial Day, flags blazon the sky.
The Mustn't Boy of Muscatine
waits in a melon patch
for shadow, scythe, and rind to shine.

Wedged in sandy crevice,
squashed like a winter bee,
he taps nervous foot in pursuit
of the Viceroy of Vitamin C.

The nearby Crenshaws spot him,
consider to weather-warn local officials;
but he's got thick flesh,
lower casabas; this boy is special.

Oh, sure, he gets a little gourd
when time dies on the vine;
but like Schulz' thumb-sucking Van Pelt
he believes in visitation of Rind Divine.

Come, central-seed cavity,
dense-net casing, prominent ribs.
Cut to ripening rites of summer.
Kid, bring your spittoon and bib.

Some say, Mustn't Boy is a crouching
misdemeanor, maid-rite felon.
He knives in reply,
Sally, want some melon?

Lend Me Your Ears

An O'Brien County Poem

Fronds, Roastin's, and Kernelmen,
Lend me your ears!
Gather round this back-forty platform!
I think you'll find my speech,
well, ear-resistible;
for I'm throwing my cob-hat
into the political bin to be
The Mayor of Maize, Ombudsman for Corn.

Tell me your acres and payin's.
Tired of being stalked,
your voice husked,
life's nothing but one big tassel,
leaves of green
exposed to such corn smut?

Corn is King!
Why, my silk amigos,
you beef the meat,
you feed all nations.
Elect me! Take the Primghar path!
Resurrect popped dreams!
I'll take on the Bushel Administration.

Brutal July's! Brutal July's!
Gives us Aurora's conditioned,
not conditional air.
Seize her! Seize her!

When harvest comes,
we give our lives;
yes, we give our lives—
in the international billions!
Talk about genocide, cereally.
Does Mother Earth truly know
how much our grasses have
tried to please her?

From soda pop to the frozen pizza—
as syrup, fodder, sensible ethanol.
Without us, succotash,
well—it would just suc!
And sodium chloride, step side!
Of this Earth, corn is the salt.

Highest Point in Iowa
An Osceola County Poem

Herbert's ascent to the Oval Office,
Sanderson and Gable, wrestling gods, who for supper, pass the Olympic torch,
Drake Relays' baton dressed in April's best weather,
Feller's perch of strike three's, dearth of ball four's,
Bourlag's bumper prize for peace, soil that's tops,
Wallace at the right wheel of FDR,
A stadium screaming to the ghost-gallop of Kinnick,
A peanut, a possibility, discovers George Washington Carver,
Ottumwa's Carol Morris, Miss Gorgeous, atop Miss Universe,
Big trouble in River City, Willson's blare of nearly four-score horns,
Prehistoric mounds, you animals, caged in underground effigy,
Bushels upon bushels upon bushels of corn,
Carrie Chapman Catt, Bloomer's no-repent bleed for suffrage,
Robert D. Ray leads the way, or perhaps tea with seated First Lady upon Terrace Hill,
Executive wisdom of a man called Cooley,
A dentist and sister whose smiles give Mona Lisa the chills,
Lewis and Clark validate future parking along the Louisiana Purchase,
Julien Dubuque first to settle here among Spanish-lead mines,
A Pulitzer scoop by the *Register* or Wells' Blue Bunny,
Laotian refugee boats find our arms open, Godspeed, and kind,
Johnny Carson's one for the road; Hayden's run for the roses,
A thespian of westerns and wars calling his career *True Grit*,
Glenn's Tennessee train; Ringling Brothers with dancing bear trained,
Des Moines, a premium place, insured under a dome of 23-carat,
What is the highest-point in Iowa? What's up between twain rivers?
What elevates Hawkeye hearts to apogee-degree?
1,670 feet in the air —
Why, you can see Seminole Territory from here —
The Sterler Farm near Sibley.

Page Boy
A Page County Poem

Pardon me, but
Mattie Lou's chattie boy was, no doubt, top trombone,
first musical chair,
among Wilson's *76*, cut above the rest.

Glenn banged the *big* in *band*,
saturated *chat* in towns from Clarinda
to anywhere Tennessee,
put a whole country in the mood — never let it slide.

Miller was Nooga-good;
Benny knew him.
Brass and woodwind, pair of Swings
to whip the Depression, restore roarin' glory.

Born to March, 1904.
Glenn Miller died flying high, 1944,
a genius deporting.
How fitting he peaked at Top Forty.

Virgin Mary at Grotto of the Redemption with Baby Jesus
A Palo Alto Poem

Here, in this castle, this cave of antimony and jewel,
the Virgin Mary awaits, salvation in arms.

Man of all men,
Stone of all stone.

Let us enter, you and I, for that is what humans do —
they go in.

Here, press this carbuncle in your palm
as we search the lapidary's palace, blind as we are, press and bleed.

Never has darkness known such light —
never descent afforded such lift.

Strip of garments, wear only the water passing your eye.
Strip all secular thought. Let prayer, redeeming wonder, amass your mind.

Here are the grottoes, such monumental tithes.
Prowl with me, alley creature, among Jesus' nine lives.

There, in cavern of choice, Mary ascends between ruby and sapphire,
above Purgatory's redolent ways, desecration, Satan's bluest fire.

Wed to heaven and earth, naked devotion her ring,
she gestures us to dig for an underground spring.

Here, friend, accept Father Dobberstein's trowel —
deeper and deeper — at last, healing Higher Ground.

Look up and look out — what vision, more miraculous than this —
as if we were with Bernadette of Lourdes, sighing Ave Maria's first kiss.

The babe cradled in pearl of her bosom — appears —
the Immaculate leads us to the cross' last station, Carrara stone tomb.

Here, she redeems us, silence rises, ecumenical tongue —
with no need to say — for Death did not enter that mournful day —

Who here among you, killed my son?

From the Desk of Josiah Bushnell Grinnell
A Plymouth County Poem

Dear Horace,   *1800s*

I have tucked your advice, headed leeward.
My *Go West* voyage ends at this Plymouth rock of sorts.
No fluked migrations on this pilgrimage—
Nothing but flat, finless land to report.

Oh, yes, some families here live like Kingsleys.
Dandelion minions puff to service in bucolic yards.
Field astronomer that I am, I've discovered Neptune—
And, yes, Merrill, Oyens, Craig—
The three moons sailing around Le Mars.

But, here, in Westfield, I mule in cement.
The pick and pan of further west will have to wait.
Don't fret, brother.
I plan to plant the Garden Greeley
Replete with wildflowers, golden and sealed.

Ah, unusual highs,
These breaths cause one's breath to bate.

I hesitate to emigrate
From such a blissful state.

Respectfully yours,

Young Man

Last of the Disney Girls
A Pocahontas County Poem

Film in the can
Disney sends her reeling
Walt's wunderkind
Willow of her 1600s self
A curve here, some blush there
She is model-squaw
Tyra of the Chesapeake banks
Supra-teen transformed from original truth
Her rings around green tree being only
Eleven or twelve
This is *Poca*hontas of the First Syllable

Or leave behind
Princess of the Box-Office Swamp
Consider her, Ambassador of Feathers
Diplomat in deerskin dress
Handshake here, guided tour there
Colonial spy for fire
Turncoat or treatisette
Her fresh-fires for sale
Sparing Smith's gullet
With a political kiss
This is Poca*hon*tas of the Second Syllable

Or place her moccasin sole in God's hands
Born Matoaka, Angel of the James
Descended daughter, root of Virginia
Spirit, arbiter, precursor of Lincoln, King
War-Score Address here, Drum-a-Dream Speech there
Sacred land, ethereal cinders delivered
To the white hand
On a sermon's wing
All oppressed hit dry land equally
Those awaiting them live free
This is Poca*hon*tas of the Third Syllable

Or perhaps
Girlfriend was out for herself
Her marriage to Governor Rolfe
Like her wedding frock, tobacoo stained
Bored with the Powhatan here, *Little Wanton* in England over there
She enshrined as Lady Rebecca of England, then smallpoxed
Just spoons from union to wealth's silver service
London Company to Disney's Magic Kingdom lunch box
Poc spoke as Rebecca, *I do* to tobacco and tyranny—Rolfe replied, *I do, too*
This was all their coupling needed to ruin onlooking Spain
This is Pocahon*tas* of the Fourth Syllable

Last of the Disney Girls

Disney-dismally mythed or Malibu-ed?
Little wilderness girl lost?
The teeth to be Mother of Our Country?
Using native reverse psychology to show who's boss?
God's spiritual sister?
On early 17th-century mission, deliverance divine?
Or perhaps We the People should throw Poc
First Society's First Ladder—for her simple braids to climb?

Floppy Dish
A Polk County Poem

Unhushable puppy, that Floppy,
Big-mouthed beagle in a box,
Pound puppet, born from balsa wood,
And one lovingly knit red sweater —
In 1957, his master Duane Ellett
Unleashed him on WHO-Channel 13,
The mutt was a natural,
Amidst those makeshift sets —
You never saw him blink —
By the 1960s, Floppy was a staple,
An after-school snack at 3:30,
Best babysitter to the bone,
You could count on him, 1 to 10,
More than your teacher or friends —
Sick days were not in his contract,
And his sitting fees, reasonably free —
He had his occasional co-star,
Uncle Taffy, Standeen, Scary Mary,
The Inspector, Matilda the Bookworm,
And a few rivals, up north in Ames,
Betty Lou Varnum's *Magic Window*
With Catrina Crocodile and Gregory Lion;
But he never was one to growl about ratings — Beep his nose —
He thought the Nielsen's was a show on prime time —
Never angered, only a child's kiss made our brown best-boy blush —
And Channel 8's Mary Brubaker, girlfriend, now you know,
Upon you Floppy dished a Capital Crush —
Unlike other legends of the screen —
Carson, Wayne, Russell, and Reed —
Floppy didn't take his talent one paw out of the state,
Like a certain cat to his favorite flakes,
Iowans young and old thought Duane and pal were more than ok,
In fact, it was the public, we humans, who barked, picketed
When executives pulled his 30 minutes
And millions of moppets' jokes off the air —
Outside beleagured station in downtown Des Moines,
Mothers in enraged curlers, babes in Floppy T's and underwear —
Thanks to Floppy, America had the biggest pencil in the world —
And cars weren't just cars, those rods rode hot —
His giggles were cold milk and warm cookies on a mundane afternoon,
Thanks, Mom and quality televison, that really hit the spot —
Floppy was Prince and Fido, but mostly Fido was King —
Duane Ellett had not something, but someone extraordinary up his sleeve,
And Floppy, the Pinocchio puppy, had central Iowa on a string

Bluffing

A Pottawattamie County Poem

Council Bluffs—
The city is one trolley car
And perhaps a golden gate away
From hedging the claim—
San Francisco of the Midwest.
Its streets throw curves at you
Like a Giants or A's pitcher.
The bluffs themselves
Gather up enough wagons
To prospect the West,
Before bowing, gently,
To the bend of Big Muddy.
If you're walking Haymarket District,
Listen to your tender loins, your legs.
A tibia or fibula may be shaking.
If ever western Iowa broke off
From the remainder of the state—
Earthquake—this escarpment is it.
Blue lamplights along Main Street
Look as if Poseidon's fish hooks
Washed ashore from a Pacific bay.
High on a hill
Croons the Grenville Dodge Mansion,
Just waiting for Tony Bennett to tea.
The fog is deceptive,
Rising from aged railroad depots
To mine through the shafts
Of the World's Oldest Dairy Queen,
Lincoln's Golden Spike,
And the Fountain of the Death Angel.
It's a comparison to the City by the Bay
At which you could shake a Kanesville.
C. B. even has an Historic Oakland Avenue.
Why, the place could turn
Amelia Bloomer into a California girl.
Just bluffing.

Near Marker 83, Westbound, Interstate 80, Illinois
A Poweshiek County Poem

A cell phone could have saved her,
but heroic grasps of US Cellular, Sprint,
arrived too late.

She spelled her *T-a-m-m-y,*
the old-fashioned way, you might say —
like Debbie Reynolds' ballad of 1957,

yet cornstalks are not cottonwoods,
so no dreamy vegetation whispered to a hoot owl,
Alert state troopers of her swoop.

A college student at Grinnell, missing,
bright-head back to the grind, August 1992,
the Pontiac T1000 beaten by heat; help, not on the way.

The discovery of what seemed to be her body, coroner's enigma:
Green eyes of the dead turn brown, blonde fronds to auburn —
and so went her spring and early features, dyed and dead for winter.

Her teeth told part of the story. *It is I. It's me.*
Identity confirmed among case-breaks of Missouri.
Tammy Zywicki had transformed, mutated,

become someone else, underneath yellow sheet,
blanket bound, red-duct tape kissing the missing co-ed goodbye,
500 miles away from the abandoned T.

Her running shoes, still gone; most doubt the aglets got away.
They, a trophy perhaps, success of stealer's field. Women look, today,
in fear of her abductor, eighteen-wheeling along concrete call, open season.

Her abductor. *Have you smoked it again, stud? Switchgrass.*
Taken another jewel of the prairie to chicory ditch?
Snuffed a second soul of worldly breath?

What good is a white- or red-flagged antenna — waving to a passerby
stranded by his own motor-mind mantra — *Floor it. Ignore it.*
Once raising a hood of hope, Tammy left all rubberneckers

an octave of screams, one for each fatal wound, coroner counted,
seven in the chest, one in the right arm.
She yells, hollers, cries, shrieks, shrills, wails, caterwauls, banshees.

An octave of screams —
Can you hear her now in your nightmares, grease?
Can you hear her now? Good.

U, Ungulate of Unequal, U
A Ringgold County Poem

Untried travelers may mistake
U-shaped street signs in the
Unsung town of Kellerton, Iowa, as
U-turn prompts
Unquestionably
Uh-
Uh.
Ununsually gifted Frank E. Jackson
Unhorsed all challengers
Upon pitching fifteen world horseshoe titles.
Ushering their hometown hero to
Unparalleled permanency,
Utilitarian and aesthetic citizens
Uplifted these long stobs for each neighborhood.
Upheaved blacksmith booties never had it so good.

Carting Them Off
A Sac County Poem

He began as most linebackers do,
a grocery boy, stock piler, market, Sac City, Iowa—
hauler of cans, flanks of meat—
taking them out, each Saturday night
to someone else's backseat—
made him strong, durable,
feisty, and hungry for Pete Rozelle
to offer Sack 'em Mac an NFL contract.

Quarterback down, bit gauzed,
longs for sea, smell of salts.
55 leans down, lean, behind line of scrimmage
offers two types of bandages,
kindly asks the sacked passer,
Miss, would you like paper or plastic with that?

Brush with Sage
A Scott County Poem

It must have been a sagebrush,
three-toothed at its tip,
whispered in William's ear,
Wild Bill, come with me.

It must have a been a desert thorn,
a runaway from somewhere Sierra,
told antebellum Billy,
I'll make you the first international star, kid. Wait'n see.

It must have been a breeze of burr,
spurring up a frontier circus,
showed Cody the bronco back-crackin' way,
how to hide buffalo, pit and fire feral game.

Indeed, it must've been a brush with sage,
roping the founding Father of Rodeo,
learned him to play *Cowboys and Indians* for pay —
Then again, folks, it might've been fame.

Brown Study
A Shelby County Poem

Entranced, enamored,
deep in thought,
sits Dane atop
the blistered and bladed
Copenhagen Taj Mahal—
Elk Horn's Danish Windmill,
a flower-flabellum
upon which he squats
to count and contemplate
his Dana's enthrall.

Foursome vaned,
fly-wheel frame,
a gift shop at mill's
tourist base—
a glacial break
of Royal C plate
colliding into Bing & Grondahl make
fails to import him.

Is the girl a match for his wares?

Oh, love's conundrum,
reverie's stare-knot—
how does our Denmark dude
connect panel-to-petal dots?

To be adored
from Baltic to North Sea shore,
Den's mulled mind must keep in store—
blade number even, pluck of four.

To pick good luck,
best to begin
with ill-fated phrase, pluck one—
She loves me not.

I Am with Woman

A Sioux County Poem

Mrs. Abe DeVries assists in the births of 206 children, 1874-93.

The cry of a birthing woman
causes the wolf's skin to curl.
I lay the ladle down, gather my 'bouts,
bring a baby into the world.

It wasn't like this in the Netherlands,
a Dutch couple settled for a bud or two.
Like grease in the fry, Americans multiply.
My, such a heap of melting-pot stew!

If the bit's one of metal, it's a sterile utensil.
All shoes, sharp and silver, fit.
206 and counting, my pink and blue fancies bouncing—
indeed. I'm confident.

I stand and deliver—come cold, drizzle, shiver,
or warm ways of ready fire.
A mid's hands are made to steady and lave;
a man's, to mend barbed wire.

Easy. Breath. Water bears to a steam.
I am nurse to my own doctor, Intuition.
I am Queen of the Queasy. *Breath. Easy.*
Instructs this Princess of the Parturition.

I am with woman. Shut the door. Leave with bed sores.
New life will be served on a folded-arm plate.
Into the 20th-century, babe, we go. If census numbers are low,
don't blame me for the staggering state.

Bust of Persephone
A Story County Poem

In your VEISHEA bonnet,
tear gas stains upon it…

Hair laurl'd in spring,
prepared to wake
Earth's slumbering air,
Persephone rises, midriff,
waist-high, pauses
way of the Underworld
to catch upsurge breath.

A square of bath paper,
truant tulip,
hit 'Seph at fore gaze,
her April ascent
bosom-blooms, Lincoln Way, Ames.
Beauty stops beastly traffic, Grand Marshal
a-float the VEISHEA Parade.

Frat boy breasts Hades' Lady a beer.

Vet offers a mint shot;
Engineer, a boilermaker;
Industrial Scientist,
some concoction, 50 proof;
Home Economist preps her
ever-clear home brew;
Agriculturist, ethanol on the rocks.

Dionysus to daffodils!
Atlas—er—at last,
Persephone's torso is tanked.
Our Dignity of Myth, sprung, unglued.

She becomes murmur of the indecipherable,
road-head reveler, rib-deep in the whoopla,
bronzed, drunken, uncouth.
A seizure of cops nabs Demeter's daughter,
cuffs her curls, smack-dab in front of the All Charities' Booth.

Story authorities whisk her in bonnie-weather jacket, straight.
Poor Per's blood-level incites a riot, exceeds .08.
Grapplers assist, take her downtown Nevada,
for no matter how immortal or statuesque—
in this metered world, Persephone tips legal limit.
Party girl is under a wrest.

Killing Two Birds with One Butter Cow

A Tama County Poem

At the Iowa State Dairy of Dreams,
Atop Norma Duffy Lyon's bovine-in-butter,
Sits a Meskwaki Native American;
Beneath the jersey greased grazer,

a
sta
cko
fpa
nca
kes

————————

Greatest Attractions on Earth
A Taylor County Poem

I GRAVITY, IOWA

The hands of
Gravity's town clock—
Snapdragons! Snapdragons!
That heavy-topped flower,
And an apple
Drops
On the hour

II OF A BARN

The owl chutes from the door
Hoot-alerts the lull yard,
For, at last, I have done it—
Hit, the broadside of a barn

The fiddle picks its way
From the bale, implements dance;
At last chance, like a plush duck,
I have won it—the broadside of a barn

An arrow bull-eyed in my back,
Hooped iron for a head,
All my life, I have been my own target,
Then along comes the broadside of a barn

The cock stirs, acknowledges accuracy,
Awakens dropped stock, dead muse of the field—
Hope acres no more. Great Zacs! I've done it—
Hit, the broadside of a barn

Grieving in the Promised Land
A Union County Poem

A break so bare, snow is hungry,
threadbare,
but thick with thin women,
rib-serious children.
The winter of 1850 reaches
wheezing branches
of New Zioneers who remain.

Mormon men have gone marching, Mexican-American War.
When infant Iowa hears of a hero, she gives his name to a county.
The women of Smith warm the prairie wool with their breasts, upper knees.
A husband's return is blessing; survival is bounty.

Spring corn has refused its silks.
Buckwheat harvests none-the-flower.
Creek, a dry throat. Open groves are open graves.

Hell in a handcart.

Angel Moroni carries wings of breadcrumbs,
her aura, a pigeon, along Saint's Passage.

Driven like the Pottawattamie from pipes in the East,
—the Called, the Chosen, the Cold—
shield with suffering sticks the wintry blind.

It is the season of the sated cemetery.
What plots await beneath the timberline?

Moses, is this the Promised Land, Mt. Pisgah,
you, too, envisioned—
Biblical mountain, way-station to God?

Ah, but to a tumbled settler, no all promises land well.

Strained timber is familiar, rings the inevitable, gives last leaf.

A woman, a child dress of zero-solstice quarter,
blue sting of December.

The unhemmed hands spool prayer.
The needled ones thread grief.

General Mills

A Van Buren County Poem

If the Pope can visit Iowa, why can't Napoleon?
Let's invite his legend, set the brigadier up
in fine bed-and-breakfast, retreat upstream,
a pebble's thrust from Bonaparte village proper.

Meredith Willson could lead the way, 76 French horns down Main Street
with its 21ˢᵗ century accolades.

A local church could become a bit confused
and serve Neapolitan ice cream,
a deft kid parting the chocolate form the strawberry and vanilla,
like Napoleon separated armies of Wellington, von Blucher.

La Petit Caporal could *bon vive* for 100 days—
the guest of *beau coup* receptions, regalia.
The Emperor-General would be *pantaloon*-proud
of this once blink-and-miss town,
puff pastry nestled inside the heart of Midland's bakery bib.
His right hand secluded beneath lower left ribs,
Nap'd admire the village's grit and its grist
to preserve past and present—just as it is.
The Louisiana Purchase—a guy's buy—
who among us didn't have an ancestor bid?

And the grind, daily grind, of both mills, *deux moulins*, flour and wool
skipping to the riverfront's water loo…

Surrender his heart, not a beat to still him.
Give Bonaparte the key, o, fairest of tiny cities.
If he stoops to conquer Keosauqua, we kill him.

The Prince Awakens
A Wapello County Poem

Before my rest in red-earth,
I shook white hands in sweet accord, peace.
Now, seize of the Sauk, flight of the Fox,
Capture my dreams and run with my sleep.

It is a stretch to state such stout neglect.
It is a yawn to claim posthumous pains.

City of Bridges, River of Mounds,
I am Chief Wapello, displeased with wake's sound.

It is about the integrity of names.
It is about the negotiation of words.

City of Bridges, River of Mounds,
Black Hawk still has ears that speak about town.

It concerns which dress cloaked a truth at 1842 council.
It concerns whose dare sat where in authority's chairs.

City of Bridges, River of Mounds,
Trapped is the territory upon trammeled ground.

It is mistreatment shroud around treaty.
It is that removal remedied the stead-settled here.

City of Bridges, River of Mounds,
Time is a liquor best dispensed by heart's pound.

It is my agency to cross the last river I wove.
It is the grave elm that weeps upon my stone bed of disbelief.

City of Bridges, River of Mounds,
Oh, Black Hawk, my brother, Sauk precedes in Fox in annals of grief.

Above the Road a la Mode
A Warren County Poem

First balloon boasted lattice-crust country apple.
Second wind stalked the view with a wince of rhubarb.
Third air enveloped a slice of threeberry —
blue, rasp, and boysen — stacked above Carlisle yards.
Fourth entry sported a tart of lemon.
A fifth sprang meringue, toasted coconut.
Number six burned a bushel pick of wild cherry.
Up and away, floated a flamed French chocolate.

The clouds' plate surely sated.
Its attic-basket, belly, firmament-full
when a patched gasser the shade of pumpkin
vined the other pieces in an *All Together, Pull!*

An eight-skirt of served desserts, even God tables a sigh.
Wishful thinking comes to Warren County. Look at that pie in the sky.

— for the John Burrell family

Truant Apostles
A Washington County Poem

They scatter like Noah's crows—
Twelve Mennonite boys—
Counted disciples, truant apostles.
The *Bibled* belt from Church—
Beyond pew-rows of bean—
To the summit of all-acres forty.

They break like a black gate—
Hats brimmed with joy—
Past cross and plow—
Footrace for grace.
Busting at heaven's seams,
Rush-heavy, the hearts *lean* for God's glory.

Inn of the Six-Toed Cat
A Wayne County Poem

The term for you is *polydactyl.*
Let's sit a spell and chat.
You say you will have me for breakfast.
Well, bed my scratch and brow!
Inn of the Six-Toed Cat!

No roll for me, I'm on a diet.
The milk is whole and fat.
Set in your ways. You've seen butter days.
Inn of the Six-Toed Cat!

I heard your first life rode with Jesse,
Silent member of James.
Obocock Bank robbed, Gang wouldn't stop
For a fur ball on Main.

You alleyed your way to Allerton.
Nothing matter with that.
Paws on door. Stay a decade or four.
Inn of the Six-Toed Cat.

How fitting it was in 1909
Rail hotel took first bat.
Brides and grooms, choose from 9 rooms.
Inn of the Six-Toed Cat.

Back to you, mitt, sorry.
History is such vex.
So…which one? Finger? Thumb?
Extra pinkie, index?

Mmm. Ghost claws are under the table.
Your grin tells me to guess.
I pick the one that can open cans.
Well, I'll be…I'm impressed.

Is this where Jennings Bryan's fire spoke?
Where Helen Keller Sunday-brunch sat?
You're living in original tin!
Rug the apologies, dearest cat.

Can you spell Chautauqua?
Instinct tells me you can't.
Did Edgar or Charlie lip better tips?
All fours. Love the décor. Inn of the Six-Toed Cat.

Gypsum, Scamps, and Beliefs
A Webster County Poem

It's a post-bellum story; some argue as fable.
If you wake a sleeping giant from his gypsum bed,
expect to find fraud at your breakfast table.

1868, when a minister's words presumed stable,
one don of holy cloth spoke of giants in the earth-red.
It's a post-bellum story; some argue as fable.

A jade named George Hull just couldn't take sermon to cradle.
He hired some muscle east of Fort Dodge to slab a ten-foot sulfate god.
Folks, expect some calcium with your fraud at that breakfast table.

Job complete, stone monster sent eastbound, *Cardiff, New York* on the label,
to brother-in-law Stub Newell, who buried hoax, shady-in-waiting, as said.
It's a post-bellum story, (but where are the animals) if this is a fable?

One year later, Old Stub reckoned he needed a well to make farm more able.
Some three feet down, diggers shouted, *Jee-rusalem! Look at that spread!*
Boys, set your shovels a plate, expect fraud at your table.

The press swarmed the find like fit flies, cable-to-cable.
Hull and Newell confessed nothing; Iowa's most solid citizen, like the case, rests.
It's a post-bellum story; some argue as fable.
Wake a gypsum giant, expect fraud at your breakfast table.

Snowbirds Drive 65

A Winnebago County Poem

To live in Winnebago, you must be
retired, gold-watched, wage-pipes at peace
with *Honk! If You're AARP* a peacock
mounted on your well-insured fender.

You must be tagged by time,
punch-clock flogged, aged, sublime,
feathers ruffled a bit,
for life is a bender.

You must be able to tow,
two-bedroom, half-bath in snow,
as you gaggle-gather in down gray,
wheel north for the winter.

Winneshiek Peaks, I and II
A Winneshiek County Poem

I   VESTERHEIM

Without trunk or tankard,
yet infinitely inspired,
He creates, paints
magenta and salmon petals,
mid-air, suspended —
like brushed angel hair,
a jar of genius,

            East

West

passion to home,

strokes of spirit
amidst the mists
of lavender, dusk-blue swirls.

No, skate, you're not dreaming —
Yes, this is Iowa —

And that starved artist over there is God

rosemaling the world.

Winneshiek Peaks, I and II

II FESTINA SESTINA

The poem comes here, Festina, Iowa, to look for lost things,
St. Anthony of Padua Chapel at vespers. A ministry,
a silence, tells well-traveled verse of sorrowful misses.
Here, sad woman moons, too, rests reject's breath, a crestfallen veil.
Author of Despair, she has pressed the Poem of Wounds on a postcard.
A bluebird, a borrowmaid, attend through a stained window.

Evening, no vacancy for tears to occupy windows.
She weds the script in hand to a dry read—things
only a heart might say for a prayer or a postcard,
each word, an act of serving, requisite ministry.
A slant of hail presses rice on the church, weather's veil,
slant empathy for a Miss who missed her *Mrs.*

The poem is priest, clears collar to speak. Discouraged clergy misses
its chance to wake prohibitive ears shut like a deaf window.
Lilt bells of nature, wind's hymns, invoke to no avail.
The sermon folds to her list of more pressing things.
Brief altar spreads Lilliputian limbs, permits Lacelady to enter its ministry.
Dark the guest descends. Poem on the floor, she'll send it a postcard.

Pin drops the church. Curses in cursive press the postcard.
Best Ann and Beak beveled at peep's view, borrowmaid misses
the train back to bouquet. Bird's echo, winged ministry,
dirges to maidy-in-waiting, *Oh, well, blue belle, all window
seats taken.* It's time to pack repair among dimunitive things—
groom on the tiered cake, sincerity crushed in teared veil.

Glass couple wages that nun's wimple-wage awaits the bereft, a vail
for one who vows to deflower the past and smoked roses on the postcard,
to press them underneath her jilted rib where, one day, ridiculous things
will stir hurt's tucked paper garden, stained on delivery. He who dismisses
her now must pay its one-sent packing stamp. The ghostly window,
the sanctuary pass curfew's last fuse of ministry.

She's not her old self, presses borrowmaid in two-minute ministry.
Alas, flits the bird, *down gown must don a new cloth, miter's veil.*
Both forget—the church has a road; lost souls have a window.
Newlyshed air grooms a way out the door, flight fit for a postcard.
It will hit brush-bride someday; it's a chance moon of misses—
moon for youth's lovers, fresh targets, blistered sweet nothings.

Things will care less, once the depressed loses the veil.
Small ministry of fallen verse wishes for crisper, uplifting postcards.
For now, she finds she misses, not the man, but opportunity—the window.

Letter from United Flight 232

A Woodbury County Poem

July 19, 1989

Dear Advice Columnists:

Question:

All three hydraulic systems down,
a stormy witch spells with her broom.

Surrender, steering! So long, elevation!
All on board destined to die!

I am most able captain.
I am least able passenger. What do we do?

Signed,
Two of Sioux City Doomed

Answer:

Don't forget.
Faith is its own etiquette.

First, pray for flat land—God's abundant lay in Iowa,
not even the bluffs roaming the river can deny.

Then, think as long as you can—
This aircraft is spirit.

You keep it as long as you can—
in His clearest blue sky.

The Egg Nog Hour
A Worth County Poem

Her county, the North Star of Iowa,
back scratch to Minnesota,
gated green for summer,
legend of winter wheat, storied in the wind.

The county farthest north in Iowa,
by most counts,
the one closest to Christmas—

So, here in Worth,
the tale of Little Ethel stirs
like the egg nog she prepared
for father's first break in the field.

He must've had a history of ailments.
The drink must've done him good long ago.

At 10 AM, The Egg Nog Hour.
Even a man got morning sickness.
Daughter looked to the frostless window.

Eggs beat, sugar added, vanilla extracted,
nutmeg grounded to scent and cream.

Her mug to the glass, the girl searched through
what she saw of summer. Fustian shirts on a wire,
uncommon loon crossing state line.

Dad was an aching tree, just hours after sunrise,
a trunk of troubles, rooted in the tum.

Daughter knew the out-of-season remedy,
off holiday, with Mom's supervision—

No parts brandy, to all parts love.

Fli*ghhhh*t of an Emblem
A Wright County Poem

It wasn't a kitty, wasn't a hawk
that propelled O. H. Benson,
grade-A Wright brother,
to spin for leaves, give Clover Club its flying start.

Behind thinking ears of children, the green buzz begins.
Bake for the blue ribbon, comb the steer with pride.
Finish your chores this coated winter morning
& we'll head for the fair, come sweat of July.

In robust veins of youth, the verdant surge begins.
Follow the feed ratio; keep your passion on fertility's prize.
In a rain's shake, bigger steers from better seeds are born
if your heart is loyal to the must of the field, trust of the sky.

Upon the calloused clap of a chap, a found project begins.
Build it with practical trees, son — ones forthright & wise.
Learn by doing — cloth, cooking, & corn.
The hands of your elders open as tutors & guides.

With muscled revival, a fresh blade begins.
Live your days in spirit, girl — breads of your labor, like the bulb rise.
All is well with the world — my how its orbit soars —
kept & flexed in good health, for the next generation of 99 voices, 99 lives.

99 Notes

Money Talks,
An Adair County Poem

Jesse James and his gang— brother Frank, Clell Miller, Bill Chadwell, and four Younger brothers— conducted the world's first moving train robbery and the first train robbery west of the Mississippi, near Adair, Iowa, July 21, 1873. The gang believed gold was on board the Chicago, Rock Island, Pacific Railroad locomotive en route from Cheyenne to Chicago; instead, they settled for the passengers' cash on hand.

The Shining,
An Adams County Poem

Born October 23, 1925, Corning , Iowa, Johnny Carson hosted the late-night talk show
The Tonight Show from October 1, 1962, to May 22, 1992, replacing Jack Parr and preceding Jay Leno.
Carson taped over 4,500 episodes during his 30-year run. The poem contains phrasal allusions from
Stanley Kubrick's film *The Shining* in which *H-e-r-r-r-e's Johnny!* is a comical, terrifying part of one scene.

Gilded Woods,
An Allamakee County Poem

Considered one of the finest hiking areas in Iowa, the Yellow River Forest began as part
of FDR's New Deal, public works. Blessed with golden autumns and array of flora (the endangered jeweled shooting star, pine) and fauna (deer), the forest is part of the Driftless Area, the rugged NE section of the state, known as *Little Switzerland*, least affected by glacial activity. Rivers, like the Volga, Upper Iowa, and Turkey flow east and west in this quadrant of the state. The poem contains allusions to the
Effigy Mounds National Monument.

A Chief When a Child,
An Appanoose County Poem

The first Native American to inhabit present-day south-central Iowa, Chief Appanoose, whose
name is Sauk for *a chief when a child*, was a gifted orator, peacekeeper who represented his Sauk and the Fox (Meskwaki) tribes in Washington, D.C., before Congress during the Black Hawk War of 1832. Appanoose County is also known for its coal industry; I am proud to say my father worked hard in those mines.

Plow in Oak, Oak in Plow,
An Audubon County Poem

During the Civil War, a farmer left his plow by an oak to join Union forces passing by. He never returned. Gradually, the trunk absorbed all but the tips.

Braille Bytes,
An Benton County Poem

Founded in 1852, the state's second oldest educational institution (University of Iowa is first),
the Iowa Braille and Sight Saving School serves the vision impaired. The musicality for the poem's first part receives inspiration from the holiday classic *Do You Hear What I Hear*. Poet Ezra Pound in his *ABC of Reading* wrote that musicality (melopoeia), imagery (phanopoeia), and logopoiea (logical meaning, dance of the intellect) are the three essential components of American poetry. Musicality is often lost to the music industry, but song originated in verse.

Portrat of Chief Black Hawk, I and II
A Black Hawk County Poem

Great warrior, leader of the Sauk during the early 19ᵗʰ century when the lands known as today as the Midwest were part of the Louisiana Purchase, Chief Black Hawk (1767-1838) was a adamant foe and fighter against white encroachment onto Native American soil. In 1832, he attempted to re-cross the Mississippi River to homelands of Wisconsin and northern Illinois, instigating, the Black Hawk War. Dismayed by treaties, constant push of federal government, and cheating trades (like the subject of this poem—a barrel of tobacco and a barrel of salt for some Iowa soil). The Black Hawk Purchase, named to humiliate the great chief following the war, enabled the government to acquire the eastern 1/3 tract of Iowa. The speaker of this poem is a Sauk after Black Hawk's death who must settle for a poor trade and head west.

Glow Depot
A Boone County Poem

Considered by many Iowans to be the greatest hero/heroine in state history, 15-year-old Kate Shelley crawled across the 184-foot-wide, 700-foot-high Des Moines River Bridge during a storm, flood-ridden night of July, 6, 1881, to warn rail officials at Moingona Depot that the Honey Creek Bridge had collapsed, taking a pusher train with it, killing two rail inspectors and injuring two more. Kate's trek over the remaining bridge was on hands and knees as the cross-ties were 3-feet apart to discourage walking. Kate stood just above 5-feet tall. Shelley's efforts saved the lives of nearly 200 passengers and crew who were to travel the across the washed-out bridge within the hour on a midnight train from Chicago. The Moingona Girl Scouts of Iowa are named in her honor.

The Buck of Wapsipinicon River
A Bremer County Poem

Buck Creek is a ghost town in Bremer County and so receives the distinction of being the deer hunting poem. The place lies just east of the waters. Some Iowa maps still show it. This poem is a tall tale or legend of sorts. It is a narrative told in rhymed couplets.

Independence Mental Health Instiutute
A Buchanan County Poem

Independence is one of four state-mental health institutions in Iowa; the others are Mt. Pleasant (the oldest), Cherokee, and Clarinda. Woodward and Glenwood also provide resource centers for the mentally ill. The speaker in this poem may or may not be a present or former resident, perhaps in a state of denial or criminal derangement.

Painting Rembrandt
A Buena Vista County Poem

The city of Rembrandt receives its name from the 17ᵗʰ-century Dutch painter Rembrandt van Rijn, famous for self-portraits and intricate use of light. A gorget is a necklace of armor worn during the Baroque Period. *Buena Vista* is Spanish *good view*. The poems is a variant sonnet and fictional ekphrasis (a poem about a painting of the City of Rembrandt, which doesn't exist).

The Whole County Did It
A Butler County Poem

The goal in this poem is to mention every town in Butler County as a possible suspect in a mock murder. Obviously, the title and concept of the poem are from the phrase, *The butler did it.*

112

Manson Killer
A Calhoun County Poem

June 28, 1979, the town of Manson, Iowa, fell victim to an F4 killer tornado, leaving 3 dead and destroying over 100 homes. The weather tragedy was 10 years after the serial-murderer Charles Manson rampaged Hollywood on a lethal run and 5 years after the book *Helter Skelter* hit the bestseller lists telling of Manson's diabolical exploits. This verse is a physical poem in the shape of a funnel or tornado.

Ascent of the Blackbird
A Carroll County Poem

Private Merle Hay was the first Iowan and perhaps the first American to die in WWW I. He died in France. His first name, Merle, is French for *blackbird*. This poem is a French sonnet and contains several French words and phrases popular in America.

The Other House of Hitchcock
A Cass County Poem

The Underground Railroad ran through Iowa for 100 years, 1838-1938, offering transportation, housing, and seclusion to hundreds of slaves. The UR entered Iowa at the southwestern tip of the state in Tabor and extended to Clinton. Lewis, Iowa, Nishnabotna River, and the George Hitchcock House were three primary resources. The poem contains allusions to the films of Alfred Hitchcock as well.

Hooverville
A Cedar County Poem

The 31st president of the United States, Herbert Hoover took the executive reins as America entered the Great Depression. Much of the blame fell on the man born in West Branch, Iowa. Hoover was a hard-working, mulit-talented person: statesman, engineer, and humanitarian. He accepted no salary to lead our nation.

Death of a Music Man
A Cerro Gordo Poem

Buddy Holly died in the same Iowa county Music Man's Meredith Willson's was born. He last performed at the Surf Ballroom in Clear Lake, Iowa. The poem's setting is just days after the plane crash. It is Valentine's Day, 1959.

Cherokee Lullabye
A Cherokee County Poem

The Cherokee tribe is not indigenous to Iowa, though many Iowans have heard of the Trail of Tears spreading from southeastern United States to the Oklahoma badlands.

Won't You Marry Me, Hill?
A Chickasaw County Poem

I knew quite early in the project that the Little Brown Church in the Vale near Nashua, Iowa, was to be its county's poem. Actually, the song *Church in the Wildwood* existed before the building, which celebrated its 150th year in 2005, the year I wrote many of these poems.

Rural School Comin' Down
A Clarke County Poem

The rural school system in Iowa was once spotted with dozens of one-room buildings throughout the state. My mother was born in Clarke County and recalled how the schools dispersed along a grid of 12 townships, 9 schools per township. Thanks, Mike Perry, for the suggestion.

Bogenrief
A Clay County Poem

You have to read or listen carefully to catch the world famous Clay County Fair in this verse. The main subject is the beautiful Bogenrief glass of the Spencer area, stained-glass windows, and the center of this poem, Tiffany lamps.

Guttenberg: Pearl Button Workers' Union Strike by Land
A Clayton County Poem

Nearly 100 years ago, Guttenberg (as well as Muscatine) was home to one of the biggest pearl-button factories in the world, fasteners made from clam shells. The town receives its name from Johannes Guttenberg, founder of the printing press. The opening line in his dedication.

In Old New York
A Clinton County Poem

Formerly knows as New York, Clinton, Iowa, rose to power in the lucrative lumber industry along the Mississippi by the 1850s. Folks heralded it throughout the country as the *City of Millionaires,* including such eminent kingpins as Chauncey Lamb and David Joyce—17 millionaires in all.

Mrs. Milk and Cookies
A Crawford County Poem

Born Donnabelle Mullenger, in Denison, Iowa, January 21, 1921, Donna Reed became one of Iowa's most beloved and adored actresses—winning an Oscar and starring in the wholesome *Donna Reed Show.* She also played Mrs. George Bailey in the perennial favorite, *It's a Wonderful Life.*

Unhappy Hour ant the Hotel Pattee
A Dallas County

The Hotel Pattee is one of the finest hotels in Perry. (Don't miss Squiers Manor in Maquoketa, the Blue Belle Inn in St. Ansgar, or the The Abbey in Bettendorf either.) Across from the Hotel Pattee elegantly sits the Thymes Remembered Tea Room. This poem is a romp connecting the two prides of Hometown Perry.

Mr. & Mrs. Wilson
A Davis County Poem

Kate Shelley is my favorite Iowa female hero, and Attorney Jonathan Wilson, who grew in and around Bloomfield, Iowa, is my favorite male hero. Jonathan is a tireless champion of human rights in the state and puts dignity in everything he does. The poem is a bit-parody on the *Dennis the Menace* comic strip as the next-door Wilsons had no children. This may be why.

Among the Brome of Autumn
A Decatur County Poem

Pheasant hunting pervades throughout the state, and my home county of Decatur is no exception. The season in Iowa begins around Halloween or All Saints' Day. Brome is woodland or meadow grass where pheasant hide and brood.

And the Explorers in This Corner
A Delaware County Poem

The book had to have a corn, cattle, hog, and, this, a wrestling poem. Iowa City, Ames, and Manchester are three Wrestling Capitals of Iowa. The town of Manchester is very supportive of the U of Iowa's Wrestling Team and sports good teams themselves. This is a tag team match of unlikelys.

Snake Alley
A Des Moines County Poem

Called the crookedest road in the world, Snake Alley in Burlington, Iowa, slivers down a lovely hill. This is a physical or visual poem in shape of the road. The words read forwards and backwards.

Voices from the Spirit Lake Massacre, I and II
A Dickinson County Poem

On March 7, 1857, one the worst tragedies in Iowa (Villisca axe murders is the other) occurred. Sioux Chief Inkapaduta and his band of Wahpehkute Dakota Sioux terrorized the Rowland Garland cabin and four other steads, taking 4 captive, including 13-year-old Abigail Gardner, released some 84 days later. Miss Gardner witnessed the slaying of her entire family. *Middle Border* refers to the Iowa, Wisconsin area.

Dream Acres
A Dubuque County Poem

Former baseball scout W. P. Kinsella's book *The Iowa Baseball Confederacy* safely hit the screen as *Field of Dreams* (1989). The poem also refers to other aspects around the Dubuque area, *brew* for the beer industry, *shot* for Shot Tower, *lead* for the Lead Mines of Spain.

Meteorite Sandwiched Theories
An Emmet County Poem

The biggest meteorite found in North America sandwiched itself north of Estherville on May 10, 1879; it weighed 437 lbs. This poem confuses meteorite with maidrite, a sandwich invented in Muscatine County, 1926, by Fred Angell, whose name appears in the poem.

The German Immigrant
A Fayette County Poem

The German ethnicity is, by far, the most populous in the state. I thought Oelwein was German, but learned it has Italian heritage. Fayette sounds French. Nevertheless, the Germans are in every county. Even Oelwein has nearly 50% German heritage.

A Tractor Is Born
A Floyd County Poem

In 1907, the word *tractor* is coined near Charles City, Iowa as the soil-treading plowing device first termed in 1901 as a *gasoline traction engine* by Charles Hart and Charles Parr seems to be a mouthful.

Geneva Talks
A Franklin County Poem

No, this poem is not about the World Trade Organization's Geneva Talks in Switzerland, though it does have some fun with phrase. The town of Geneva, Iowa, of course, is the source for verse.

Anything for a Buck
A Fremont County Poem

Sidney, Iowa, is home to the world famous Sidney Rodeo and a dirt museum. The poem extends the metaphor of being bucked of a horse to being bucked of a marriage.

How to Sway Popular Opinion
A Greene County Poem

Pollster George Gallup was born in Jefferson, Iowa. This is a concrete poem in the shape of a ballot.

Hog Ghost Story
A Grundy County Poem

I've heard it said that Iowa has more pigs than people. It is not even close. The state raises nearly ¼ of America's pork, ranking 1st in hog inventory. I chose Grunt—er—Grundy County for the hog poem for its sound. If you take the word *hog* and the first two letters in *story*, mix them, you get *ghost*. The poem is a bit Dickensian, after Charles Dickens, in honor of author Herbert Quick, author who grew up in Grundy.

Admit One Bandit to Yale
A Guthrie County Poem

The Raccoon River and Valley run through Guthrie County. The county also provides a touch of the Ivy League, the town of Yale.

Kantorville
A Hamilton County Poem

Novelist MacKinaly Kantor, who won the Pulitzer Prize in Fiction for *Andersonville*, was born in Webster City, which is not in next-door Webster County. The poem is a precursor to the novel, set in an imprisoned baseball field, one like you might have seen at the Southern Civil War camp.

Hobo Convenience Store
A Hancock County Poem

Each August in Britt, Iowa, hoboes around the nation gather for the Hobo National Convention. The poem is an extended metaphor comparing life in a boxcar to working in a convenience store.

Mr. State Fair
A Hardin County Poem

Bill Riley, an Iowa legend, started the Iowa State Fair Talent Search in 1960. His nickname says it all.

Bertrand Lets Off a Little Steam
A Harrsion County Poem

April 1, 1865, was no Civil War April Fool's Day for the folks aboard the *Bertrand*. The big boat sank while turning a bend upon the Missouri River near Missouri Valley. All survived, but few remembered where exactly the steamer headed to deliver goods to Montana prospectors sank. In 1967, salvors found the steamers packed with preserved supplies.

116

Ode to Thresher
A Henry County Poem

The Old Threshers' Reunion is in Mt. Pleasant, Iowa, the weekend over Labor Day.

The Almost Bride of Hayden Prairie
A Howard County Poem

With nearly 240 acres of untouched grasslands, Hayden Prairie in northern Iowa is our state's largest natural prairie. The poem includes Russian and Slavic characters; the village Protivin is Czech.

A County Seat So Small, It's a County Sat
A Humboldt County Poem

Dakota City is the smallest county seat in the state. I utilized county-seat libraries throughout Iowa when writing the book. I had to go to Humboldt, Iowa, for the library in these parts.

Cattle Call or Cream
An Ida County Poem

You find *IDA* in the family name for cow, *BOVIDAE*. Ida County gets the cattle call.

Amity of the Amanas
An Iowa County Poem

You'll find all gravestones facing east in a cemetery in South Amana. It's silent and breathtaking. I sat here many times while journeying around the state. All stones are uniform and inspiration for the poem in form of a sonnet.

It's the Girl from Andrew, Sister
A Jackson County Poem

This is the first poem written for *99 Voices, 99 Lives: County Poems of Iowa.* I was visiting my friend Jack, when I noticed RAGBRAIers coming into the town of Maquoketa. I thought if they can travel the state, so can I. 6-on-6 girls' basketball had a great influence on my life. Andrew guard Kim Peters is my favorite player of all time. It is an honor to write this poem for her.

Maytag, You're It
A Jasper County Poem

This is a lonely satire, for obvious reasons. Our thoughts and prayers to all Maytag employees.

Conversation with Ferris Wheel Descending
A Jefferson County Poem

Are you going to have a State Fair poem? Several people asked me this from 2004-2006. Yes, but you'll have to look in Hardin and Jefferson counties. This concrete poem is in the shape of a ferris wheel, as folks in separate seats are trying to have a conversation. The first State Fair was in Fairfield, 1854.

The Smolder of Old Stone
A Johnson County Poem

Our first state capital was Iowa City. The capitol building beautifully stands today on the campus of the University of Iowa. The building burned, November 20, 2001, destroying the dome.

Knock on Wood
A Jones County Poem

Grant Wood's *American Gothic* is perhaps the world's most recognizable painting. His sister, Nan, and dentist B. H. McKeeby posed as farm couple in 1930.

Ache, Woebegone, Daze
A Keokuk County Poem

My favorite town title is What Cheer, Iowa. What better place for a poem about the blues?

German POW at Algona Camp
A Kossuth County Poem

A few things blew me away while writing the poems, including discovering Iowa had prisoner-of-war camps for Germans during WW II. This is a macabre look at life inside.

Civil Bells
A Lee County Poem

Oh, yes, Iowa had one Civil War battle. It was in Croton, Iowa, and involved nothing more than a few cannon fire over the pond.

Quaker Notes
A Linn County Poem

I actually like oatmeal with raisins and brown sugar very mush, or much. This poem is a tribute to one of the state's finest food industries, Quaker Oats.

Great Flood of 93
A Louisa County Poem

We are still drying out from the inundation of water of 1993. SE Iowa was hit the hardest. The poem is 9 stanzas long, 3 lines per stanza — for '93.

Let It CIO, Let It CIO, Let It CIO
A Lucas County Poem

Labor leader and founder John Lewis was born near Lucas, Iowa. Present-day AFL-CIO originates, in part, back to him.

Children of a Lesser Sod
A Lyon County Poem

I had a very emotional time writing this one. The Orphan Train rode through Iowa for almost 100 years, 1854 to the Great Depression. The train placed out nearly 10,000 orphans in Iowa. The Delmar Depot (Clinton County) served as an inspiration for the poem, placed in the upper corner of NW Iowa as if the train is pulling out of Iowa for the last time, and the kids want to stay.

What's Heating Coffee Cups at the Northside Café?
A Madison County Poem

The Bridges. John Wayne. Red Delicious. Take your pick. I picked all of them for the poem.

Mulogy at the Cemetery for the Union Crossbred
A Mahaska County Poem

Buried mules that served in the Civil War. You find them at the Nelson Pioneer Farm just north of Oskaloosa. I couldn't resist.

The Dutch Letters of Your Mind, I and II
A Marion County Poem

Pella, Iowa, was home and nerve-central to me when writing the book. The first part of the poem contains all images appearing in the town's Klokkenspel. The second part was inspired from the 2 statues in Scholte Gardens, *The Gardener* and *The Gift*. Thanks to Pella High School, Pella Public Library, the Fettys, the Yoders, the Tripps, and the Kleins.

Three Centerpieces
A Marshall County Poem

It is at the center of our state. State Center is the Rose Capital of Iowa.

Ferryspeak
A Mills County Poem

The book is obviously nostalgic. Ferry, make way for bridge.

Hanging with Hamlin Garland in Watts Theater, Osage, Iowa
A Mitchell County Poem

Born in Wisconsin, died in Hollywood, author Hamlin Garland wrote his Middle Border series in Iowa. The Watts Theater is one of the state's finest cinemas.

Loess Hills
A Monona County Poem

The Loess Hills are unique soil formations found only along Iowa's western border and a province in China. So, how do you write a poem about soil, dirt? When in doubt, a love song.

Buxton Wonders
A Monroe County Poem

Now a ghost town, Buxton, Iowa, thrived as a coal town and place of prosperity, equality for African-Americans, including fantastic pro-like baseball teams.

Villisca Axe Murders
A Montgomery County Poem

With its electricity out, Villisca, Iowa, woke the morning of June 10, 1912, to the news of a mass murder at the Joe Moore home. All 6 members of the family and 2 little-girl guests were killed. The murderer used Joe's axe, cleaned it, and left it at the site. No one has been convicted.

It's the Great Melon , Muscatine
A Muscatine County Poem

A take-off from the cartoon Halloween classic by Charles Schulz.

Lend Me Your Ears
An O' Brien County Poem

A bit of Shakespeare in the corn poem. Why O'Brien? Look at the corn fields there. Wow!

Highest Point in Iowa
An Osceola County Poem

A list poem of some of my favorite accomplishments in Iowa. Other Iowa FYIs —
Polk, most populous; Adams, least populous; Lee, lowest point; Kossuth, largest; toss up for the smallest.
Iowa ranks 9th among states in total number of counties.

Page Boy
A Page County Poem

Band leader Glenn Miller was born in Clarinda, Iowa, 1904.

Virgin Mary at Grotto of the Redemption with Baby Jesus
A Palo Alto Poem

Father Dobberstein gave 42 years of his life to building this amazing Grotto, one of my
favorite places in Iowa — 9 grottoes portraying the life of Christ and redemption of Mary.

From the Desk of Josiah Bushnell Grinnell
A Plymouth County Poem

I chose the county farthest west to acknowledge the *Go West, Young Man* advice
of Horace Greeley to Josiah Grinnell.

Last of the Disney Girls
A Pocahontas County Poem

This verse considers four theories surrounding the life of Powhatan native Pocahontas,
who, in her early teens, became a love object and guide to Englishman John Rolfe in pre-colonial US.

Floppy Dish
A Polk County Poem

Our most populous county, Polk County offered a number of options: State Capitol,
insurance industy — This one is for Central Iowa baby boomers who knew this guy as noontime
friend and after-school babysitter at 3: 30 — Floppy and his pal Duane Ellet.

Bluffing
A Pottawattamie County Poem

This poem is an extended metaphor comparing Council Bluffs, Iowa, to San Francisco.

Near Marker 83, Westbound, Interstate 80, Illinois
A Poweshiek County Poem

The abduction and subsequent murder of Grinnell College student Tammy Zywicki,
August 1992, put fear in motorists for over a decade. The poems considers if technology might
have saved her life. Grinnell is known as Jewel of the Prairie.

120

U, Ungulate of Unequal, U
A Ringgold County Poem

Known as the Filly Slipper Pitcher and Grandfather of Horseshoes, Frank Jackson of Kellerton, Iowa, won the world's first horseshoe pitching championships in 1909. The 15 lines in the poem are in honor of his 15 world championships, each beginning with a capital *U* like a horseshoe. *Ungulate* referes to hoof-shaped.

Carting Them Off
A Sac County Poem

The verse has fun with the word *sack.*

Brush with Sage
A Scott County Poem

Born in LeClaire the same year Iowa became a state, 1846, Buffalo Bill Cody became America's first international star with his Wild West Show, and, without questions, Iowa's most famous native of the 19th century.

Brown Study
A Shelby County Poem

A brown study is an intense look, observation, or contemplation at something as this fellow is doing on top of the brown Danish windmill.

I Am with Woman
A Sioux County Poem

Midwivery was perhaps the last subject I ever thought would be in *County Poems of Iowa.* Mrs. Abe DeVries assisted in the births of 206 children, 1874-1893.

Bust of Persephone
A Story County Poem

Look for the word VEISHEA spelled in acrostic verse (downward) in the poem.

Killing Two Birds with One Butter Cow
A Tama County Poem

What a pleasure to meet to Butter Cow Lady, Norma *Duffy* Lyon, in person. Thank you, Norma, for sharing your exquisite gifts.

Greatest Attractions on Earth
A Taylor County Poem

Gravity, Iowa, and a big round barn.

Greiving in the Promised Land
A Union County Poem

The Mormon Trail across southern Iowa was often a hard one — dissension and rough winters. Many Mormon men had to serve in the Mexican-American War of the late 1840s, 1850s. Mt. Pisgah is a lovely stop in Union County.

General Mills
A Van Buren County Poem

Bonaparte, Bentonsport, and Keosauqua are villages in Van Buren County worth the visit.
This poem is a play on the word *Bonaparte* as if Napoleon were visiting the city.

The Prince Awakens
A Wapello County Poem

Nicknamed The Prince, Chief Wapello of the Fox was a more peaceable man the
Chief Black Hawk of the Sauk. He died shortly after signing treaties with the whites.
Ottumwa is known as the City of Bridges.

Above the Road a la Mode
A Warren County Poem

The National Hot Air Balloon Classic in Indianola, Iowa, August, was an obvious choice.

Truant Apostles
A Washington County Poem

This poem was inspired by a postcard I saw at a Kalona general store — Mennonite boys breaking
from church with enthusiasm.

Inn of the Six-Toed Cat
A Wayne County Poem

The bed-and-breakfast poem. Cat with an extra claw roamed the premises for years.

Gypsum, Scamps, and Beliefs
A Webster County Poem

It's a strange but true story about a giant carved from Ft. Dodge gypsum. The poem
is a villanelle.

Snowbirds Drive 65
A Winnebago County Poem

This poem needs little trailer.

Winneshiek Peaks, I and II
A Winneshiek County Poem

The Vesterheim Museum in beautiful Decorah, Iowa, is America's largest Norwegian museum.
St. Anthony of Padua Church in Festina, Iowa, is deemed the World's Smallest Church. St. Anthony is
Patron Saint of Lost Things. The second part of the poem is a sestina, a difficult form.

Letter from United Flight 232
A Woodbury County Poem

This poem is written in letter from as if from the crew and passengers aboard United Flight 232,
which crashed in Sioux City, July 1989. It is an advice column in honor of Dear Abby and Ann Landers,
twin sisters born in the county.

122

The Egg Nog Hour
A Worth County Poem

My good friend Kent Fetty says this may be the most obscure poem of the batch. It's based on a true story about a mother and daughter, who each summer morning, would prepare egg nog for Dad as he pulled his tractor up to the house on a break from chores.

Flighhhht of an Emblem
A Wright County Poem

Superintendent O. H. Benson designed the 4-H emblem in the early 1900s after watching school children playing in fields of clover. Look for the head, heart, hands, and health in the poem.

Villanelle for Iowa's 160ᵗʰ Birthday

Drink in the candled hour—enjoy eighth score.
Fair state, who plates the world, both husk and horn.
Age you must, blessed assured, 'tis grace adored.

As glaciers gave way to flesh, field, and stone,
Natives tilled earth-eternity, first corn.
Drink in the candled hour—enjoy eighth score.

Oneota clouds, dusk-herd, passed sky and floor.
Beautiful land—geode, oak, ditch rose—torn.
Age you must, blessed assured, 'tis grace adored.

Firstborn, Free State, bled through Mexican War.
Mississippi, Missouri, Big Sioux formed
borders for drink, this hour—enjoy eighth score.

Bring heritage to event, nothing more—
a circus, a bike race, and apple core.
Age you must, blessed assured, 'tis grace adored.

What suits you, state? Your gifts we're present, sworn.
Ready for confetti? Finch, flick gold horn!
Drink in the candled hour—enjoy eighth score.
Age you must, blessed assured, 'tis grace adored.